2

ENGAGING THE CULTURE, CHANGING THE WORLD

The Christian University in a Post-Christian World

PHILIP W. EATON

IVP Academic

An imprint of InterVarsity Press
Downers Grove, Illinois

InterVarsity Press
P.O. Box 1400, Downers Grove, IL 60515-1426
World Wide Web: www.ivpress.com
E-mail: email@ivpress.com

InterVarsity Press® is the book-publishing division of InterVarsity Christian Fellowship/USA®, a movement of
students and faculty active on campus at hundreds of universities, colleges and schools of nursing in the United States
of America, and a member movement of the International Fellowship of Evangelical Students. For information
about local and regional activities, write Public Relations Dept., InterVarsity Christian Fellowship/USA, 6400
Schroeder Rd., P.O. Box 7895, Madison, WI 53707-7895, or visit the IVCF website at <www.intervarsity.org>.

All Scripture quotations, unless otherwise indicated, are taken from the Revised English Bible. Copyright © Oxford
University Press and Cambridge University Press 1989.

Exerpt from "The Dry Salvages," Part V in FOUR QUARTETS, copyright 1941 by T. S. Eliot and renewed
1969 by Esme Valerie Eliot, reprinted by permission of Houghton Mifflin Harcourt Publishing Company.

While all stories in this book are true, some names and identifying information in this book have been changed to
protect the privacy of the individuals involved.

Cover design: Cindy Kiple
Interior design: Beth Hagenberg
Images: Seattle Pacific University/Jimi Lott

ISBN 978-0-8308-3929-2

Printed in the United States of America ∞

Library of Congress Cataloging-in-Publication Data

Eaton, Philip W., 1943-
  Engaging the culture, changing the world: the Christian university
in a post-Christian world / Philip W. Eaton.
      p. cm.
  Includes bibliographical references and indexes.
  ISBN 978-0-8308-3929-2 (pbk.: alk. paper)
  1. Education (Christian theology) 2. Education—Philosophy. 3.
Teaching—Religious aspects—Christianity. 4. Learning—Religious
aspects—Christianity. 5. Universities and colleges. 6.
Postmodernism—Religious aspects—Christianity. I. Title.
  BT738.17.E28 2011
  378'.071—dc22

                                                            2011006806

P	19	18	17	16	15	14	13	12	11	10	9	8	7	6	5	4	3	2	1
Y	27	26	25	24	23	22	21	20	19	18	17	16	15	14	13	12	11			

CONTENTS

PREFACE AND ACKNOWLEDGMENTS

AT THE BEGINNING OF HIS 2005 BOOK about Paul, the gifted and prolific New Testament scholar N. T. Wright comments that he is "conscious that every paragraph could attract footnotes to itself like wasps round a jar of honey."[1] I echo this sentiment heartily. As I venture into these reflections, I am in debt to a whole shelf of wonderful books and writings, and of course to a host of terrific people I am blessed to call friends, family and colleagues. And so I begin these reflections with an almost overwhelming sense of gratitude, and I hope this will be the note that rings clearly from every page.

I sit in front of a sizeable stack of very good books on higher education, each articulating with passion and clarity the purpose and value of the modern university. It all begins in 1852 with Cardinal John Henry Newman's monumental *The Idea of a University*, that great legacy statement for all such thinking on the modern university. I think also of Jaroslav Pelikan's fresh and challenging look at Newman's vision, called *The Idea of the University: A Reexamination*, an urgently needed update on the idea for our time. I think also of Stanley Hauerwas's provocative reflections in his 2007 *The State of the University: Academic Knowledges and the Knowledge of God*. These are the kinds of books that shape my understanding of the nature of the

---

[1]N. T. Wright, *Paul: In Fresh Perspective* (Minneapolis: Fortress, 2005), p. xi.

university and its significant role in modern society.

But these and so many other writings begin to surface some of the limitations of the dominant model of the secular university, which has evolved over the last century and a half. As an answer to some of these limitations, I will lift up a vibrant alternative: the idea of the Christian university. As Hauerwas says so succinctly, "If Christians are people with an alternative history of judgments about what is true and good they cannot help but produce *an alternative university.*"[2]

Because of my lifelong investment in Christian higher education, my stack of influential books includes several important contributions on the idea of the Christian university, or more accurately, the Christian *college.* The classic in this vein is *The Idea of a Christian College*, a wise and influential book by Arthur Holmes, or more recently, Duane Litfin's *Conceiving the Christian College*, both expressions out of the same tradition—indeed, both from the same institution, Wheaton College. I must mention as well Mark Schwehn's reflections in *Exiles from Eden: Religion and the Academic Vocation in America*, a book that set me on a path some years ago to think in new ways about my own vocation.

My hope is to take things in a different direction, seeking to strike a new note in this chorus of thinking about the rich tradition of Christian higher education. I am convinced we have entered a new day for the Christian university. I believe we must reconceive the Christian college. Christian universities must think hard about what it means to embrace the Christian story, even in a world that calls such stories into question. We do our work now in a post-Christian world, negotiating the new terms of exile in which we find ourselves as Christians. We must affirm the story of what is true and good and beautiful, our ancient Christian story, right in the midst of a culture that has grown profoundly suspicious of calling anything true. We must think hard about how to marshal the considerable tools of the university to address the desperate needs of an urban, hurting, confused, rapidly changing, but exhilarating world in the twenty-first century.

The days of the comfortable, intellectual journey carried out safely

---

[2]Stanley Hauerwas, *The State of the University: Academic Knowledges and the Knowledge of God* (Oxford: Blackwell, 2007), p. 91. Emphasis added.

in the middle of circled wagons are over. There is no room for separatism for the Christian university of our day. There is no room for the ivory tower of intellectual formation alone. We must engage. We must enter into the swirl of our post-Christian culture. We must learn better how to influence the culture from the position of exile. This venture is fraught with all kinds of challenges, but what an exhilarating venture it can be.

Yet even after expressing my gratitude for the influential thinkers and friends who have shaped my thinking about Christian higher education, I find myself veering off in a different direction of influence. I believe there is a new sphere of thinking that must inform our understanding of the Christian university. I am thinking of theologians and biblical scholars and Christian intellectuals, especially, for me, N. T. Wright, Lesslie Newbigin, Richard Hays, Walter Brueggemann, Pope John Paul II, Jürgen Moltmann, George Weigel, Rich Mouw, James Davison Hunter and Richard John Neuhaus. A compelling thread weaves together these various thinkers: the notion that the call of the Christian gospel requires, imaginatively and actively, to engage the culture. They also share the vision that intellectual and theological formation must translate into practical, relevant action—the call to make the world a better place through the transforming gospel of Jesus Christ.

Of course, it is not only the reading, study and reflection that provide the backdrop of influence for these pages. I am very grateful for the encouragement, support and patience of so many people over time. First I thank my extraordinary colleagues at Seattle Pacific University, those who have partnered with me every step of the way as we have tried to shape a relevant, responsive vision for our university.

In particular, I thank my dear friends and colleagues on the President's Cabinet: Marj Johnson, who has listened and responded thoughtfully to most of these ideas before they went "public," as well as Don Mortenson, Les Steele, Bob McIntosh and Tom Box. I also thank my able and competent assistants, Karen Jacobson and Kristin Hovaguimian, for always picking up the slack when I most needed them. Thanks also to Jennifer Perrow for her careful readings of the manuscript and for offering helpful comments, corrections and bibliographic guidance, always with good cheer and enthusiasm.

I am blessed to work with an outstanding faculty at Seattle Pacific. So many of them are the models for the kind of university I am defining in these pages. This faculty is among the best in Christian higher education. I am especially grateful for my teachers and friends in the School of Theology. My thanks also to a competent and loyal staff, who surround and support the enterprise of higher learning—the ones sometimes overlooked for their enormous contributions.

My three sons, Mark, Michael and Todd, and now their spouses, have all helped me engage the issues of life and love and culture. Thanks also to my sister, my two brothers and their wonderful spouses. I am exceedingly grateful for family discussions and debates and discoveries throughout my life. The influence on Christian higher education from this group of people is remarkable, and I am deeply grateful to them all.

I thank most of all my wife, Sharon, a patient listener over so many years, willing to listen again and again to my ideas with a gracious smile, willing to bring me back to earth with gentleness, strong encouragement and support, and even sacrifice of her own. Because of Sharon, my thoughts—and who I am—are more concrete, relevant and sensitive to the real needs of people.

Finally, my parents gave me the gift of knowing I live in God's huge, unfolding drama. At the core of their being, they knew that God would make all things right in the end. This is the hope in which I was nurtured. I also came to know that this hope is not for me alone. These two strong and faithful people taught me that I have an extraordinary opportunity to participate in God's grand narrative *so that* all of God's children might flourish. For this I offer my deepest gratitude.

INTRODUCTION

THE CHRISTIAN UNIVERSITY IN A TIME OF EXILE

Christian believers are now, more than ever—spiritually speaking—exiles in a land of exile.

JAMES DAVISON HUNTER

Is there anyone among you who, if your child asks for bread, will give a stone?

JESUS (MATTHEW 7:9 NRSV)

IN HIS 2010 BOOK *TO CHANGE THE WORLD,* James Davison Hunter reminds us that "ours is now, emphatically, a post-Christian culture, and the community of Christian believers are now, more than ever—spiritually speaking—*exiles* in a land of exile." We must "come to terms with this exile."[1] Coming to terms with exile while effectively and winsomely engaging this post-Christian culture—that is what this book is about.

As Christians struggle to understand our new location as exiles in the world, we find ourselves asking, What now? Do we rest comfortably out on the margins of influence, taking our shots from time to time, but mostly complacent and resigned with this new position of exile? Or do

---

[1]James Davison Hunter, *To Change the World: The Irony, Tragedy, and Possibility of Christianity in the Late Modern World* (New York: Oxford University Press, 2010), p. 280.

we put our distinctive story at risk by simply blending in, thereby accommodating to the new ways of a pervasive secular culture?

Most of the time, at least among the Christians I know, we find ourselves decidedly uncomfortable adopting either of these options. And so we begin to pose questions like these: Are these our only choices? Is there another, more satisfying, way? What are the competencies and skills required of us now? What new understanding about culture and the gospel do we need to develop? Is there a new posture we must assume in order to be an effective presence? Sometimes frustrated, sometimes fearful, often feeling inadequate to the task, we ask these questions as we live out our lives in this new and profoundly secular age.

Because "the presumption of unbelief has become dominant," as Charles Taylor tells us, American culture increasingly persists in pushing the gospel of Jesus Christ to the margins of influence.[2] This is a complex process that Christians feel acutely. We feel like exiles. Here is the tension: More than ever, we find ourselves believing that our Christian story of human flourishing can make all the difference in a broken, chaotic, often confused world. But we also find ourselves feeling timid, intimidated, reluctant, afraid at times, often bumbling as we try to tell our story effectively and winsomely. This is what it means to live as exiles.

And so we ask ourselves: How can Christians actually *speak* a gospel of joy, hope and grace into a culture that has grown tone deaf to the language we speak? How do we go about engaging a culture that calls all our deepest convictions into question? And then we must ask these questions: Doesn't the very heart of the gospel call us to make the world a better place for all of God's children? Doesn't the biblical story call us to confidence and action, even in this historical moment of exile? Doesn't the ancient promise of our faith—that God will make all things right in the end—obligate us to roll up our sleeves and bring healing, hope and joy into the world?

Hunter continues with these critical questions:

---

[2]Charles Taylor, *A Secular Age* (Cambridge, Mass.: Belknap Press of Harvard University Press, 2007), p. 12.

How can one be authentically Christian in circumstances that, by their very nature, undermine the credibility and coherence of faith? What is an authentically biblical way of existing within a pluralistic world in which Christianity will never be anything other than one culture among others?[3]

The answers to these questions do not come easily, and we are not always comfortable with the answers when we find them. But we must address precisely these questions if we have any notion of guiding our world in directions that are life-giving and flourishing.

━━━━━━━━━━━━━━ ■ ━━━━━━━━━━━━━━

In the pages that follow, we will try to think carefully about the role of the Christian university for such a time as this. What does it mean to be a Christian university in this post-Christian world? How does the purpose of a university change because it now serves from a position of spiritual and cultural exile? Here is my premise: The Christian university holds special promise to lead the way toward a better world, not only for Christians, but for all of God's children everywhere. The Christian university can help us regroup and can help re-equip us for this moment of exile.

What does this mean? First, it is the Christian university's job to do the hard thinking about how Christians can make the world a better place. What are the tools necessary for such an ambiguous task? What does it mean to be faithful and obedient to God's call on our universities for this time? Christian universities must help us understand that culture is critical. Our job is to be culture savvy, culture experts, and to lead the way for Christians everywhere in just these essential matters.

Second, it is the Christian university's job—perhaps its most important job—to equip the next generation of leaders to engage our culture and the cultures of the world. We need to help our students understand the power of culture. We must teach them to speak a language of healing, wholeness and reconciliation.

---

[3]Hunter, *To Change the World*, p. 224.

Third, it is the university's job to teach and to model how we embrace our Christian story, even while our culture calls into question all stories of what is true and good and beautiful. Graduates must be equipped to lead the world in better directions, precisely because they have learned how to embrace the Christian story. Our embrace must be meaningful, thoughtful and sophisticated.

And finally, we must build communities of trust and grace in which such an embrace becomes compelling, attractive and natural. There are other places where these tasks can be tackled, to be sure, but none holds the same promise as the Christian university; this alternative university is indeed the place where world change can begin.

I recently attended a fundraising breakfast sponsored by PATH, an organization in Seattle dedicated to taking the best medical technology to poor children all over the world. I found myself compelled to fill out a pledge card as I thought, *What a worthy place to give our money*—quite directly to a group that helps children who are trapped in circumstances of disease and malnutrition, which are profoundly beyond their control. PATH is making the world a better place for God's children around the globe.

Soon after, I sat at a commencement ceremony at Seattle Pacific University, listening to one of our outstanding graduating seniors present the class gift for the year. She and her classmates had decided to give the gift not to the University, not for "more benches or plaques on the campus," she said, but directly for the poor. These thoughtful students had picked out another Seattle organization, Agros, founded by Seattle Pacific alumnus Skip Li. Agros focuses on providing land for the poor in Central America, which Skip believes is the only way for the downtrodden to find their way toward self-sufficiency. Our students had decided to work with Agros to make the world a better place.

As I listened, I found myself asking, *So what about Seattle Pacific, this outstanding Christian university, this 120-year-old institution?* Are we also focused on changing the world? *Can* a university change the world?

Should that be its purpose? Are the considerable tools of the university at all relevant to the deep needs of world poverty, global disease and uneven economic opportunity? Can we bring guidance to a culture that seems to have lost its moral and ethical bearings? Do we channel the great work of the university in such a way to provide the tools for our students to build healthy lives and strong families? Can we point the way beyond the paralysis of conflicting ideologies to build thriving communities?

And one more question natural to the mind of a university president: how does the university compete for loyalty and for money with organizations like PATH and Agros that are so direct and focused on changing the world as they serve the poor? I actually worried about those benches my graduating students did not want to fund. How will we build our buildings and preserve our facilities, *our place*, to serve the vision and mission of our universities into the future?

Suddenly it came to me. Yes, indeed, world change begins *somewhere*. A vision for organizations like PATH and Agros was formed and shaped *somewhere*. The students who gave that class gift were taught *somewhere* to believe they could and should try to make the world a better place. And they were given the tools, the competencies, to address the deep needs of their lives, their communities and the future of the world.

Yes, world change begins in *a place*, a place intensely focused on shaping and influencing the younger generation in directions that are good and life-giving. We call that place a university. World change begins by equipping young people with competencies that address the needs of the world, to be sure. But world change begins in a place that is animated by a story of what is true and good and beautiful.

I have come to believe that the Christian university, indeed Seattle Pacific University, is *a place* where world change begins. This is a place that is animated from its core by a story of human flourishing—the Christian story. *Someone, somewhere,* needs to provide eager young people with *the* story of human flourishing that will guide and motivate them in worthy directions for the future of our world. I am convinced this is the extraordinary promise of the Christian university.

Jesus asked, "Is there anyone among you who, if your child asks for bread, will give a stone?" (Matthew 7:9 NRSV). With all their youthful curiosity and idealism, young people come to our universities seeking a story that can make sense of it all, a story that can guide their lives in good and healthy directions, a story that can make the world a better place. This is the *bread* they come seeking. If we give them instead suspicion and cynicism, we have handed them a *stone*. If we hand them a stone, the university has scandalously failed a whole generation; we have squandered our obligation, our responsibility and our opportunity to change the world we serve.

I write these pages out of a deep conviction that the Christian university, rightly focused and at its best, is called—and is perhaps best equipped among universities—to help lead the way toward a better world. While I know this may be a stretch for some, I hope to test this premise: *The world needs the Christian university.*

I have no illusions that the Christian university will anytime soon become the dominant model for higher education in America. So much has been done, over the last century and a half, to move our great universities in directions that are decidedly secular. I also have no illusions that the Christian university always gets it right. In addition, I have no need to launch a competitive battle between ways of doing education: the Christian way against the secular way.

Fully recognizing that the numbers for the Christian university are small compared to other institutions of higher education (though the number is growing rapidly and disproportionately); fully recognizing that the Christian university has too often indulged in damaging separatism, absurdly believing that we might influence the shape of the world by preaching only to our own choir; fully recognizing that Christian universities too often scramble to measure themselves only by the educational, scholarly and pedagogical presuppositions of secular universities; fully recognizing with some dismay that even strong evangelical Christian families send their kids to secular universities, what they perceive to be the more prestigious alternative; fully recognizing the sometimes profound failure of the Christian university to teach a full gospel of transformation for our world—recognizing all of this, sometimes with pain and regret, I contend that the Christian university stands the best chance in our time to articulate and model a vision of human flourishing that will make the world a better place for all of God's children.

The world needs the Christian university at the very least as an alternative to higher education's drift of deeper purpose. George Marsden and so many others have informed us that the university simply lost its soul over a century and a half or more.[4] While I have enormous respect for the great universities of our day and while I want to avoid foolish competitiveness, quite simply the Christian university has *something more* to offer. We do have a soul, out of which we have developed that *something more*.

And here's the reason for that *something more*: The Christian university is animated from its center by a guiding narrative of what is true and good and beautiful. Simple as that. That is the difference. At its deepest levels, our guiding narrative is the story of the life, death and resurrection of Jesus Christ. It is a story that emerges out of the ancient promise that God will make all things right in the end—a promise supremely fulfilled in Jesus Christ—and so we look back to our source.

But we also look forward. The resurrection calls us to the new creation yet to come. This is our hope for human flourishing. This is what activates our imagination to build a better world. And so we invest ourselves in the unfolding of this grand drama of new creation. Our great challenge is to know better how to *embrace our story* when all such stories are called into question by our postmodern culture. Our challenge is also to understand how this great story animates the work and life of the university. Our *greatest* challenge is to learn better all the time how to equip ourselves to engage this culture and to change our world.

---

[4]George M. Marsden, *The Soul of the American University: From Protestant Establishment to Established Nonbelief* (New York: Oxford University Press, 1994). See also James Tunstead Burtchaell, *The Dying of the Light: The Disengagement of Colleges and Universities from Their Christian Churches* (Grand Rapids: Eerdmans, 1998).

Unthinkable, foolish, even scandalous to the rest of the American academy, the work of the Christian university is profoundly shaped by the Christian story, that ancient-yet-living story of human flourishing. That's the difference. That's the alternative.

But as the Christian movement has encountered massive cultural shifts over the last couple of centuries, our Christian universities, and Christians in general, have often lost the ability to speak our story into the culture. There is an abundance of evidence that Christians have become both biblically illiterate and theologically shallow. Our voices are weak as we try to speak our story convincingly. As Hunter says, pessimistically and dismissively, "For all the talk of world-changing and all of the good intentions that motivate it, the Christian community is not, on the whole, remotely close to a position where it could actually change the world in any significant way."[5]

Christians find themselves battered and beaten to the sidelines of influence. We are often timidly withdrawing, conceding defeat, unsure about our case, unwilling to do the hard work of engaging what we perceive as a threatening culture. We lack the tools for cultural engagement. We lack the confidence. It's much easier simply to circle the wagons. Too often we shrug our shoulders in resignation at the drift of the secular culture in which we live.

We forget how powerfully relevant our story is. And we have lost a sense of urgency, mostly out of discouragement and resignation. But we must remember this proposition: Christians have a powerful, transforming story of human flourishing to share with the world, even this very complex post-Christian world in which we live.

The poets and prophets of our ancient Christian story—even in the face of deeply resistant cultures, even in exile, even in the face of death—stepped out onto the rooftops, onto the platforms of their day, with "shouts of joy," as the biblical poet Jeremiah said. Our story of gladness encourages us to sing out with joy. Our Christian universities, and Christians everywhere, must learn better how to speak our story into the culture, winsomely and effectively, speaking into a culture that has

---

[5]Hunter, *To Change the World*, p. 274.

grown tone deaf to the joy we have to offer.

Jeremiah makes the bold, imaginative claim that *God* will make all things right in the end.[6] This is the great promise that anchors the Christian story from the beginning. This was God's preposterous promise to Abraham. In God's covenant with his people, fulfilled supremely in Jesus Christ, God calls us to enter into this unfolding drama of *making all things right*. We hear the call to action. We roll up our sleeves and go to work to make the world a better place. This is the promise we are invited to embrace:

> They shall be radiant over the goodness of the LORD. . . .
> I will turn their mourning into joy,
>> I will comfort them, and give them gladness for sorrow.
>>> (Jeremiah 31:12-13 NRSV)

------------------------------------ ∎ ------------------------------------

The question in these pages is this: What if we were to build our universities on this story of turning sorrow and mourning into radiance and joy? What if we modeled this ancient vision of human flourishing for our students and for our surrounding communities? What if we were motivated in our special work as Christian universities to announce our radiant story from the platforms of our day? What if we were to see it as our responsibility to help shape the lives of the next generation of leaders for the world to "be radiant over the goodness of the Lord," to change the world from sorrow into gladness? What if this story, this promise, this joy, becomes the *animating heart* of the purpose of Christian universities in our day?

N. T. Wright says that "the gospel of Jesus points us and indeed urges us to be at the leading edge of the whole culture." This is precisely where our Christian universities must shine. This is where we need to focus our energies. And this is where the Christian university should be

---

[6]While this theological language may seem commonplace for our notions of eschatological hope, I am informed in this view by so much of the work of N. T. Wright, who claims over and over the deep Jewish covenantal roots for Christian hope. Jürgen Moltmann certainly echoes this view of Christian promise.

guiding Christians everywhere. We need to train the leaders of the future to get out there on "the leading edge of the whole culture," articulating and announcing, winsomely and effectively, the transforming gospel of Jesus.

It is abundantly clear that we will narrow our influence as Christians if we do not commit ourselves to take the gospel of Jesus right out there on that leading edge of culture. But being on the leading edge of culture will require significant new competencies of cultural engagement. We must learn a new language, a new posture of fearlessness, a new posture of winsomeness.

Our task, Wright goes on to say, is to "mount the historically rooted Christian challenge to both modernity and postmodernity, leading the way into the post-postmodern world with joy and humor and gentleness and good judgment and true wisdom."[7] The Christian university has not always seen itself in these terms, often withdrawing into a kind of unhelpful separatism, often intimidated by the culture, often scrambling to align itself with the model of the secular university. But I think Wright has it right. Our task as Christian universities, and indeed as Christians, is to be out on that edge with "joy and humor and gentleness and good judgment and true wisdom."

This is the bread we have to offer when the younger generation comes asking for bread. We've got to get this right. And if we do? The Christian university just may be the place where world change begins.

---

[7]N. T. Wright, *The Challenge of Jesus: Rediscovering Who Jesus Was and Is* (Downers Grove, Ill.: InterVarsity Press, 1999), p. 184.

ENGAGING THE CULTURE,
CHANGING THE WORLD

A University, taken in its bare idea . . . has this object and this mission;
it contemplates neither moral impression nor mechanical production;
it professes to exercise the mind neither in art nor in duty;
its function is intellectual culture; here it may leave its scholars,
and it has done its work when it has done as much as this.

JOHN HENRY NEWMAN

A critical reexamination of the idea of the university—not simply
of John Henry Newman's idea of it, or of someone else's idea of it,
but of the idea itself—has become an urgent necessity. . . .
A modern society is unthinkable without the university.
But it does seem fair to say that . . . the university is in a state
of crisis and is in danger of losing credibility.

JAROSLAV PELIKAN

THE STORY OF THE AMERICAN UNIVERSITY in the twentieth century and the early twenty-first century is one of unparalleled, unprecedented achievement. We can't imagine the shape of America or the
quality of life we have enjoyed in the last century without our universities. Without exception, our national leaders are educated in our colleges and universities. Generation after generation, the professions are

replenished with highly capable lawyers, doctors, business leaders, professors, scientists, engineers, teachers—all of whom are educated in our universities.

The American public spends 351 billion dollars a year on higher education alone, an indicator of how highly we prize our universities. Most every parent, whether a college graduate or not, knows the importance of a college education for their children; it is a ticket out of poverty, a path toward productive, rewarding work. We recognize in our universities something of immense and irreplaceable societal and personal value.

Though threatened by rising cost over the last decade or so, access to American universities is greater than it has ever been in any society throughout history. Our universities turn out well-educated graduates, hundreds of thousands of them each year. They are equipped with skills and competencies to be the leaders for our nation and the world. Our universities also produce research that changes the way we see the world, tools that we use to maintain our competitive advantage in the world, tools that enhance the personal health we are able to enjoy. While we often hear that rising nations are nipping at our heels to become world leaders in higher education, without question, American universities remain the envy of the world.

And yet there is another side to the story about the American university that has begun to emerge. Jaroslav Pelikan, one among many influential voices sounding an alarm, calls for "a critical reexamination of the idea of the university." This very *idea* was first and fully articulated in 1852 by the great John Henry Newman in his monumental *The Idea of a University*. Pelikan surveys the landscape of higher education since Newman's foundational work and declares that "the university is in a state of crisis." He goes on to say, with grave concern, that the university of our day "is in danger of losing credibility."[1]

How can this be? On the one hand, we witnessed unqualified success over the last century and more, and on the other, we hear voices like Pelikan's calling into question the very *value* of the university.

---

[1]Jaroslav Pelikan, *The Idea of the University: A Reexamination* (New Haven: Yale University Press, 1992), p. 11.

Under such scrutiny and critique, questions immediately come to mind: What do we mean by *value* when talking about the university? What do we understand a university's purpose to be? How do we calculate the value of a college education or the value of the university in our society, or the value of higher education to the future of the world?

Stanley Hauerwas says, "There are two questions seldom asked by the faculty and administrators of universities: 'What are universities for?' and 'Who do they serve?'" We don't ask such penetrating questions, he says, precisely because we "have no ready answers to give."[2] Perhaps we who live out our vocations in the university have grown complacent about making our case. Perhaps we don't even know how to address the question of value, assuming that everyone, after all, *knows*. What need is there to understand and articulate the university's deeper purpose, meaning and value when students continue to clamor to get into our revered places of learning? Or perhaps we are a little timid, even a little muddled, about the very core of our enterprise. In other words, we may not have the answers—or care to give them—just as we face a society grown restive about our cost and our value. People are questioning the very idea of the university. If we are to maintain our credibility and influence as universities, we must have answers to these questions about our deeper purpose and meaning.

■

We must begin with questions like these: Does the university equip the next generation of leaders with a story of what is true and good and beautiful? Do we bring hope into the world we serve, hope derived from a guiding narrative? Is the university providing for students and to the world a story of human flourishing, a story that will make the world a better place for all of God's children everywhere?

Here are my convictions on these questions: If our universities fail to embrace a story of what is true and good and beautiful—and if we fail to present to our students and to the world a story of hope, actu-

---

[2]Stanley Hauerwas, *The State of the University: Academic Knowledges and the Knowledge of God* (Oxford: Blackwell, 2007), p. 76.

ally to serve the world in this way—then we are failing to make a compelling and enduring case for the value of a university education. If we are failing to claim a story of what is true and good and beautiful as the *animating heart* of our work as universities, we are in danger of losing our credibility and influence, despite all the good we are accomplishing.

Having made such sweeping declarations, immediately I must contend with challenges to these driving ideas. For example, in his 2008 book on higher education, the formidable Stanley Fish admonishes people within the university to "save the world on your own time." Saving the world, making the world a better place, cannot be the purpose of the university, he contends. "Teachers [and by implication, the universities themselves] cannot, except for a serendipity that by definition cannot be counted on, fashion moral character, or inculcate respect for others, or produce citizens of a certain temper."[3] Those things must happen elsewhere in our society, decidedly not in our universities, according to Fish.

Others would argue that universities certainly *are* about making the world a better place. After all, that's the speech every university president is eager to give. What's the big deal? Of course it's true: universities always seek to equip graduates with skills and competencies to contribute to our societies; universities provide important research for the benefit of all people. Some have even argued that football teams are important forces for creating community within our towns and cities. All these are most certainly true. And they are good. But is this enough?

Some argue that aiming for any practical outcome should not be the goal of education, that learning, in and for itself, is the goal of all educational pursuits. This view contends that the shaping of the mind is the sole reason for the university to exist. As he sought to lay out the foundational idea of the university in mid-nineteenth-century Ireland, Newman was strongly drawn to this position. Although with a tinge of ambivalence and reluctance, Newman marshals an eloquent overall po-

---

[3]Stanley Fish, *Save the World on Your Own Time* (New York: Oxford University Press, 2008), p. 14.

sition: "knowledge is capable of being its own end." This is an argument we often hear, perhaps most prominently in our liberal arts colleges and the universities that have grown out of such colleges. "Such is the constitution of the human mind," Newman says, "that any kind of knowledge, if it be really such, is its own reward."[4] Be careful, he warns, of imposing practical, utilitarian, even spiritual goals on this pure pursuit of knowledge. Be careful even about training students for a profession. Be especially careful about lofty things like making the world a better place. The job of the university, Newman says, is to create a "culture of the intellect," to teach the "real cultivation of mind," to lay "a foundation for the intellect to build upon."[5] That alone should be the purpose of the university, he argues.

Later in his discourses, Newman says quite emphatically,

> The business of a University [is] to make this intellectual culture its direct scope, or to employ itself in the education of the intellect. . . . A University, taken in its bare idea . . . has this object and this mission; it contemplates neither moral impression nor mechanical production; it professes to exercise the mind neither in art nor in duty; its function is intellectual culture; here it may leave its scholars, and it has done its work when it has done as much as this.

Very often, we do indeed rest here, content that our job is complete, the university's purpose is fulfilled. For all who seek to attach something more expansive to this "bare idea," Newman cautions that the real idea of the university, its primary and even sole function, is to educate "the intellect to reason well in all matters, to reach out towards truth, and to grasp it."[6]

Can a university change the world? Should that be its declared purpose? For Newman, at least most of the time, and for Fish and others,

---

[4]John Henry Newman, *The Idea of the University* (Notre Dame: University of Notre Dame Press, 1982), p. 77.
[5]Ibid., pp. xlii-xliii.
[6]Ibid., pp. 94-95. We find, perhaps, the key to Newman's confidence in this "intellectual culture." When he says the goal of intellectual formation is to "reach out towards truth, and to grasp it," he strikes the note that distinguishes his moment in history from ours. We live in a time when all claims of the truth are called into question. Now intellectual formation must be disconnected from any such informing context, or such meaningful reward, as the truth.

the business of the university is the pure pursuit of intellectual formation. If this creates a better world, so be it. But if it does not . . . ?

———————————————— ∎ ————————————————

Who am I to argue with the great John Henry Newman? Any educator must respond to these eloquent statements of intellectual formation with resounding approval. This still must be a foundational building block of the university. But should we not ask what has happened since Newman's mid-nineteenth century, as finely tuned intellects were released from any guiding narrative about what is true? The shaping of bright minds does not necessarily lead to the shaping of good people.

I am not in the least claiming that the university is wholly responsible for the darkness unleashed in the twentieth century, but the university, over time, has most certainly contributed to the unhooking of intellectual formation from a guiding story of what is true and good. While the causes of this massive cultural shift are very complex, the university has often been on the leading edge of such change.

We rightly and enthusiastically focus on the intellectual development of our students as we prepare them to become the leaders of our world; clearly, without such intellectual preparation, there is little hope for our society. But can this be all? Can we really believe that the development of Newman's "intellectual culture" is the "bare idea," the essential core, of the university for our troubled times? Can we rest comfortably knowing that the university "has done its work when it has done as much as this"? If this alone is the driving purpose of today's university, we are offering the younger generation a stone when they come asking for bread.

But there are still other objections to my contention that the university ought to be animated by a narrative of what is true and good and beautiful. Many argue that it is impossible in our postmodern culture for the university to agree on a story of what is true. There are so many stories floating around from which to choose. When we propose that we carry a vision of hope into the world, the question immediately arises: How do you know your version of hope is hope for others?

This challenge comes from deep within the reigning orthodoxy of our culture. We are told in so many ways that we must maintain ultimate neutrality on all things that matter. We must demonstrate extreme tolerance for all views of truth, a posture that keeps us from ever making claims for any vision of human flourishing. This is a formidable challenge we must engage openly and thoroughly as Christians and as Christian universities.

Many carry this notion of neutrality a step further. To them, our highest calling as the university is to equip our graduates with a posture of *suspicion* about all claims of what is good and true. Postmodern intellectuals call this a hermeneutics of suspicion: our highest skills are interpretive, not declarative or formative. We come to the act of interpreting with extreme suspicion, if not cynicism; all texts (and people) are inherently deceitful. We who work in universities are the ones most capable of exposing those texts (and people) for what they really are. The writers of texts are motivated by power, the power of one gender or class over another, the power of the elite over the common person, the power of one faith over another, one culture over another.

Therefore, we cannot *trust*, we are told, any proposed vision of human flourishing. This notion of trust, or the lack thereof, is huge for our culture. In the end, we cannot trust any assertion that the role of the university is to bring hope into the world through an anchoring story— precisely because we cannot trust any anchoring story. We are the ones, in the comfort and isolation of the academy, who can best and most dispassionately challenge, expose and deny what others regard as true.

To strike this posture of suspicion is often regarded as the ultimate purpose of the university. We are intellectually and philosophically hip, cool, uncommitted, neutral, tolerant of all notions of truth—never settled, always searching. This is the only intellectually credible posture, we are told, the only viable posture in postmodern culture.

We need to explore whether it is possible to graduate people who know how to engage texts, ideas and narratives *trustingly* rather than *suspiciously*. As we explore the idea of the Christian university for our time, we must rediscover our commitment to trust, and that means reading the texts of our faith tradition trustingly. Developing a hermeneutics of trust looms large on the agenda of the Christian university.

——————————————— ▪ ———————————————

How do we go about embracing a story of what is true and good and beautiful, embracing our ancient Christian story—so that we might bring hope and radiance and meaning into the world we serve? As Christian universities, we need to turn our faces two directions at once. First, we must turn *inward* as Christian intellectual communities of the highest order. A commitment to genuine community is critical. We must dig deep, with vibrant and vigorous intellectual commitment, into our ancient Christian roots. We must renew our ability to teach and learn the Scriptures with theological sophistication across the disciplines. We must learn better how to gather in meaningful worship as communities of learning.

Second, we must focus *outward*, always seeking to engage the culture and change the world with our story—never, ever yielding to the comfort and security of withdrawal or separatism, either Christian or intellectual. We must commit to being in the mix, on the leading edge of our culture and cultures of the world, always seeking to be relevant, to be helpful, to be responsive to the needs of the communities we serve and the world we hope to impact for good.

Day in and day out on our campuses, we must direct our students and our scholarship and teaching in both directions: turning inward to anchor our experience of human community with our enduring story, and intensely focusing outward with a vision to make the world a better place for all of God's children. We must intentionally arrange our daily lives in the university in these two directions, even as we recognize the profound tension it causes.

As we read our newspapers each morning and witness the mindnumbing, seemingly indiscriminate carnage of war, the hatred between religions, the clash between sects, between cultures and civilizations; as we witness the ravages of poverty and rampant disease; as we wallow in our self-indulgent political and ideological dividedness; as we scramble to craft a moral framework for questions of destructive behavior, greed, technological advancement and medical research; as we wrestle with our own disquiet over how to determine what is right and wrong, what is true and good; as we witness, helplessly it seems, the volatile swirl of economic conditions that threatens to damage the world economy and even our own financial security; as we witness the mindless, soulless destruction of thousands of unborn babies; as we think hard on how to preserve the value of text in a culture gone wild with the flickering impermanence of text messaging; as Google becomes god, that spectacularly available omniscience of our day; as the great libraries, accumulated and collected over nine hundred years on our university campuses, suddenly become available on our laptops on the kitchen table; as all the resources of those libraries, the very roots of our culture, most all of the ancient texts of human flourishing, are called into question—well, this is the world we must engage, as universities, as Christian universities. This is the world into which we have the extraordinary opportunity to speak our story of human flourishing.

Our ancient story can change this world. Our story can make this world a better place. But we have a huge task ahead, a task best accomplished—or led, I will argue—by the Christian university.

THE STORIES WE TELL

THE AMERICAN UNIVERSITY IN CRISIS

Both [the church and the university] are caught today in the throes
of a situation that is difficult to describe as anything but a crisis,
a crisis of confidence . . . still good places perhaps for the young
to learn something about the past but definitely not the places
to look for guidance about the real world and its future.

JAROSLAV PELIKAN

The topics we address are circumscribed by
what I suspect are shrinkin pheres of influence.

JOHN T. CASTEEN III

The chief driver of events right now is not only globalization—the integra-
tion of economies and peoples. It's also the contest among cultures over the
power of consecration—the power to define what is right and wrong.

DAVID BROOKS

IF WE READ THE SIGNALS CAREFULLY, there seems to be a cloud of uneasiness settling down over the American university. The American academy is a little diffident, at times a little defensive, in the face of suspicion about the true value of the university. The university's constituents—students and their families, legislators and community leaders, foundations and the media, donors and the general public—are asking some tough questions: Why does a university education cost so much? Is a college education necessary for success in life? Isn't the notion of ivory-tower education arrogant, snobbishly elitist? Is the research done in universities always relevant, in touch with the needs of a real world? Doesn't faculty culture lean too far to the left, both politically and culturally? Isn't tenure a protection of mediocrity? Isn't it almost impossible for faculty to agree on any kind of meaningful change for the way the university does its curricular work?

When we ask these sorts of questions, we are searching for an understanding of *value*, the real value a graduate takes away from an education in one of our universities or the real value of a university's contribution to the quality of life in the community it serves. It is fair to ask what value we are getting in return for the enormous investment of resources both for individual families and for our society.

When we get into these moments of suspicion about real value, universities must step up with a fresh kind of honesty: "Here's what we really care about. This is what really matters to us. We've thought hard about this, and here's the true value of education we are willing to trumpet to the world."

———————————————————— ∎ ————————————————————

As universities go about the process of defining their value in the face of such challenges, sometimes there are perceptions of value that do not square with reality. We need to clear these misperceptions out of the way before we can get to any notion of real value. For example, the president of a public institution recently made the audacious claim that the costs at his university are less than those at a private university. *Oh really?* I had to ask. That is true only if he ignores the massive amount of state funding received by his institution, both for operating funds and capital expenditures. This president was claiming a value that simply does not exist.

It is often said that private institutions, like the Christian university I serve, attract only rich kids, when in fact the average family income of students in my institution is lower than the income of families at the big public institution across town. Our very sophisticated strategies for financial aid, formed over decades of practice, serve needy students very well. This is a more accurate story of value that must be told.

We need to get the facts straight about the value of a college education. It is our job—especially for those who provide leadership for our universities—to tell true stories about the meaning, purpose and practice of the university.

But beyond some of these issues of distorted perception, how do we go about determining the real value of the university? We can learn a lot about by listening to a university president talk to a group of prospective students and their parents, or by taking a campus tour with a skilled admissions officer. Some of the students who conduct tours for prospective students are perhaps the clearest voices of the university's real value. They see things with the eyes of our customers. Sometimes, they can penetrate through the smoke and the mirrors and give us a real sense of the value of the university from the ground level.

Recently an outstanding president of one of our elite institutions said that the purpose of the university is all about gathering together smart people and empowering them to think innovatively. "Smart people and innovative thinking—if you bring those two things together," this president said, "something powerful is going to happen, something good, something of great value, indeed something that will change the world." To be sure, this is one of the good stories we tell about the purpose of the university.

But is this enough? Isn't it fair to ask whether there is a guiding story that will help us determine whether an innovative idea actually serves something good among our students and in our world? Is there a framework that might help us determine if these smart people are also good people?

One story of value we often tell is that our universities, or even some of our fine colleges in more rural areas, are engines that help to drive the economic well-being of the communities in which they reside. Our universities create jobs, build buildings and support surrounding businesses; our students come, spend money, and often live and work in our communities after graduation. This too is a story of real value.

The late Myles Brand, then president of the NCAA, made an eloquent case that the football teams of our major universities build genuine community within cities and towns across America. Surely there is some truth to this value too. Universities often strengthen our communities, build loyalty and a sense of common purpose, and bring people together for common goals. This is a good story about the value of the university.

Yet another story: the American system of research universities is the envy of the world. Though we must be acutely aware that this claim is under severe contention, as other nations—in particular China and India—invest aggressively in their own universities to become world-class competitors. At a dinner table in Beijing, I sat across from the president of one of China's universities. Partially through a translator, we talked about his great admiration for the American university and the creative nature of learning in the United States—our tendency toward invention and innovation in the classroom and the laboratory. China's learning culture had been more systematic and rote, he said, an important limitation moving forward. But China's goal, this university president said, is to become the world leader in higher education.

Another story we often trumpet is that a college graduate can expect to make one million dollars more in a lifetime than someone who has not received a college degree. This is a true and commonly reported story. Our prospective students see this financial benefit as a real value of going to college. I would imagine this story makes its way into every speech given by a president to prospective students and their families, as it should.

Universities also claim that we are about the very important business of shaping and enhancing the lives of the next generation of global leaders. We are giving them the skills and competencies to succeed in life and to negotiate their place in a complex and changing world.

We also claim that universities work hard to ensure that this generation of students is as broad and diverse as the communities we serve.
Some time ago, my university hosted on our campus a group of leaders
from the urban core of our city. These were folks who know more than
anyone about the damages and dead-ends of poverty and crime on the
streets of their neighborhoods. We pledged our support, pledged our
partnership to find a way to place students from their neighborhoods
and their churches in our university. We also pledged that we would
create the support structures necessary to guide them toward graduation. We have invested our energies, our resources and the passion of our
people to fulfill these promises. If we keep our pledges on such promises, this is one of the good stories of real value about our universities.

One of the speakers at that gathering, Barbara Williams-Skinner,
made the claim from the podium that a university education is a ticket
out of poverty, that once students have received that all-important degree, they have chosen a different path in life. Doors open for them that
are shut to their peers who choose not to go to college. A college education can most certainly break the cycle of poverty. This partnership
between universities and the urban communities is vital for the advancement of individuals, for the improvement of neighborhoods and
for the health of our nation.

And so adding up all of these good and positive stories about the
value of the university, I am very comfortable claiming, in the language
of Jaroslav Pelikan, that "modern society is unthinkable without the
university."[1] This has been so in the West for some nine hundred years,
from the very foundations of the university. The university has had a
significant hand in shaping the culture and achievements of the world
toward something good. We should rightly be very proud of this noble
institution in our midst. We should do everything we can to preserve
its presence and effectiveness in modern society.

These stories of the university are the reason we continue in America
to invest billions of dollars annually in higher education. They are the
reason families continue to scramble to pay for a college education for

---

[1]Jaroslav Pelikan, *The Idea of the University: A Reexamination* (New Haven: Yale University
Press, 1992), p. 13.

their children, sometimes through enormous family sacrifice. There is true value here. The university for our day has a story it can trumpet with pride.

━━━━━━━━━━━━━━━━━ ▪ ━━━━━━━━━━━━━━━━━

Why is it then that Pelikan has written his book *The Idea of the University: A Reexamination* with the bold and disturbing assertion that "the university is in a state of crisis and is in danger of losing credibility"? As we have already noted, he calls for "a critical reexamination of the idea of the university—not simply of John Henry Newman's idea of it, or of someone else's idea of it, but of the idea itself." This, he says, "has become an urgent necessity."[2]

In his 2007 book *The State of the University*, Stanley Hauerwas says, "We are content to comfort ourselves by repeating familiar slogans about the importance of being an educated person who can think critically."[3] In other words, we simply do not dig down beneath the slogans into the deeper dimensions of the meaning and purpose of the university. We rest on our laurels. We rely on the positive perceptions of the university's value.

In this restive moment, this time of uneasiness about the purpose of the university, Hauerwas states bluntly, "I obviously think that the university as we know it is in deep trouble." But then he adds, capturing the ambivalence we find so often in these kinds of indictments, "That does not mean we would be better off without the university."[4] We love the university, its grand history, its enormous value to our society over time. But we also sense there is something missing at the very core of the enterprise, something in need, at the very least, of reexamination.

John T. Casteen III, longtime president of the University of Virginia, said of universities today and of the presidents who lead them,

---

[2]Ibid., p. 11.
[3]Stanley Hauerwas, *The State of the University: Academic Knowledges and the Knowledge of God* (Oxford: Blackwell, 2007), p. 76.
[4]Ibid., p. 32.

"The topics we address are circumscribed by what I suspect are
shrinking spheres of influence."[5] This is an enormously discouraging statement, but I suspect its sentiment is echoed by university
presidents across the country. How can this be? And why should it
be so?

Can it be true that universities and their leaders are hamstrung because of the strong forces of postmodern culture, the paralyzing notions
of political correctness, so that we can't even talk openly and honestly
about things that matter? Are we truly free to address issues of moral
choice or character formation? And if our influence is shrinking in this
way, what chance do we have of changing the world? What chance do
we have of influencing the lives of our students so that they can change
the world?

In a 2006 reflection on what he calls "the decline of the secular university," C. John Sommerville claims that "the secular university is increasingly marginal to American society."[6] In a damning assertion, he
states that "universities are not really where we look for answers to our
life questions. That is the sense in which they seem marginal."[7] Sommerville argues, not noticeably from a Christian perspective, that most
of the significant questions of life and culture involve religious dimensions of reflection, yet the academy today has all but banished religion
from its methods of discovery or terms of discourse. This is part of the
reason the university has little to say about the big questions of life.
Sommerville proceeds to outline the "very odd notion" of "the irrelevance of the secular university in America."[8]

Somehow the stories of the university of our day are not complete
enough. People sense that something is missing. Somehow we are not
addressing the deepest yearning of our students or, by extension, the
deepest needs of our society. We are beginning to ask for *something
more.*

---

[5]John T. Casteen III, "Presidential Leadership," *The Presidency*, Fall 2002 <www.virginia.edu/
presidentemeritus/spch/02/spch_presleadership.html>.
[6]C. John Sommerville, *The Decline of the Secular University* (Oxford: Oxford University Press,
2006), p. 4.
[7]Ibid., p. 8.
[8]Ibid., p. 3.

■

Some time ago I was speaking in downtown Seattle to a roundtable of business leaders and professionals on what I thought were the distinctive qualities of my university. I decided, naturally for me, to talk about the moral, spiritual and character development of our students. I used as a springboard for my comments the work of James Davison Hunter about the "death of character" in our culture, the notion that we have lost a common language about character formation, a common set of values from which to teach character. In spite of cultural trends, I went on to say, character formation is at the heart of the matter for my university. We want to be clear, as our mission statement declares, that we seek "to graduate people of competence and character."

I stated as clearly as I could that character is vitally important in our society. Surely this audience would conclude with me that character is important in business and the professions. And then I stated that I believed the university must be involved with the complex task of character formation. This is a story of universities we all can champion, I said. This is a story of true value.

When the question-and-answer time arrived, another university president raised his hand and said, "But, Phil, this is not the purpose of the university. We have no business thinking we have anything to say in the complex and conflicted arena of character. We can't be in the business of imposing any kind of moral framework on our students." I think I was being told I am somewhat antiquated in these pursuits, too moralistic, out of step with the true business of the university in our day.

Another participant posed the same question a bit differently: "Is it not true that, developmentally, there is no more work to be done by the time these students reach college age? Are they not already shaped? Why don't we just get on with the business of providing competencies and skills with which our students must ultimately address the needs of a complex world?"

I had thought I was preaching to the choir, but when it comes to character formation as a critical part of education, I began to realize there is no familiar hymn on these issues. I realized there is no choir out there. We have lots in common in our understanding of the purpose of the university, for which I am grateful, but we also find ourselves with conflicting stories about the deeper value of the university.

I think back to my experience in college. I was eagerly searching for something during this stage in life, and I was listening intently to my teachers and mentors—indeed, turning to the college itself—for a story about life. Along with the skills I hoped to master, I wanted a story that would point the way forward toward a good and meaningful life. I came to college wanting to make good choices, so that my life would be productive but also meaningful. I was asking for a story of what is true and good and beautiful. Could the college offer something like that for me?

Through my college experience I also was seeking to know whether the story given to me in my childhood was credible. If not, how did I need to modify that story, to provide the important nuances, to understand the shades of complexity, to add various dimensions that might be missing? Even with this growing sense of complexity and ambiguity, was there a coherent view of the world around which I could shape my life? Was there a view of the world that would help me understand what my own contribution to making the world a better place might be?

I came to college equipped with a worldview, shaped by my parents, family, church and schools. But I knew, at some level, that I was testing the set of assumptions I had been given, trying it out against the broad learning of the ages, pressing the boundaries and examining the assumptions of my childhood—and all of this in the context of a trusted community. Yes, I *trusted* my college. I trusted that this very college was in pursuit of the truth too. And my earnest desire, though not always understood maturely, was to align myself with a true story about human life on this planet, about human destiny, about human flourishing. I believed that this was what college was supposed to do.

I trusted my professors and the leaders of my college and even the college itself to handle my growth and maturing in responsible ways. Of course I pressed the boundaries, as any healthy college student will do, and of course I bumped into people I could not trust. Yet I still expected that this college would provide the *bread* I was asking for, a story of what is true and good and beautiful that would guide my life, a story that might make the world a better place. Wasn't it fair and right to expect that I might receive this bread and not a stone?

What if my college had decided, like the leaders in my audience in Seattle, that all this was not necessary, or that it was too complex and contested to be the purpose of a college? Where would I have turned for direction, for wisdom, for a view of human flourishing around which I might shape my life? I believe this is the *something more* students desperately need from our universities. When this *something more* is missing, decidedly absent from the core work of the university, this is precisely why the credibility of the university is being questioned.

We must rethink the work of the university for our day. And I believe we might profitably turn to the Christian university as a powerful alternative, a strong resource for providing that *something more* our students and our society are looking for.

3

NEGOTIATING A WORLD OF COLLIDING MAPS

We live in a world of colliding maps.

CHAIM POTOK

Knowing is always part of tradition. The mental activity involved in trying to make reliable contact with reality can function only by indwelling a tradition of language, concepts, models, images, and assumptions of many kinds which function as the lenses through which we try to find what is really there.

LESSLIE NEWBIGIN

Structural and cultural realities of our society in this historical moment . . . make us doubt any kind of transcending narrative.

JAMES DAVISON HUNTER

THE LATE JEWISH NOVELIST CHAIM POTOK said on my campus some years ago that "we live in a world of colliding maps." Each one of us has constructed our own little, individual story, our map, out of the bits and scraps of information we have been given. Here we are, floating around in a large universe of meaning, bumping into one another from time to time, but with very little compelling sense of connection, direction or congruence. Highly individualized maps of where we are headed, lots of collision, no big drama that holds it all together, very little authority or tradition to guide us—that's the way we might describe our view of the world at the moment. We live with "an irresolvable and unstable pluralism—the collision and conflict of competing cultures," says sociologist James Davison Hunter. This "is and will remain a fundamental and perhaps permanent feature of the contemporary social order, both here in America and in the world."[1]

I was out on Google Earth the other day, and I zeroed in on some of the complex spots on our planet. I looked down into the streets of Bagdad, then over to Tehran and on to Jerusalem. I skipped over to see the explosive sprawl of Shanghai and Seoul, and then looped over into the streets of London and New York, and then across to Seattle, where I live. There are all kinds of maps drawn down there, in every spot in the world. And we all consider that *our map* holds just the right angle on the rest of the world. People are willing to lay down their lives to defend or promote their own special map. We each believe our map to be true.

Then I pulled back and took a long look at the whole marvelous planet, this spectacularly beautiful globe, so green and healthy from this distance, floating as it is in such massive blue space. Is there a purpose here for the whole? Is there a big story that brings this entire planet together with some kind of *narrative of meaning*? Is there a story of how it came to be, how it got to be in this very place, where it is going? Or is it just floating? Must we just settle for the collision of the local maps as the final view of meaning for the earth? Is there hope for this globe beyond its conflicts?

There are so many maps within the big map, maps drawn up by geography, by deep and ancient roots in history, culture, religion. This causes us to ponder whether things like economic interdependence, discovered in powerful new ways in our century, bring us together. And do the powerful, new forces of technology bring the human community together meaningfully into a map that makes sense of it all? Or will the

---

[1]James Davison Hunter, *To Change the World: The Irony, Tragedy, and Possibility of Christianity in the Late Modern World* (New York: Oxford University Press, 2010), p. 202.

separate maps keep colliding, perhaps progressively more violently as time goes by? As we look closely at the trouble spots where maps are indeed colliding, it is hard to believe that human flourishing is possible on this beautiful, troubled globe.

The philosophical, cultural and educational orthodoxy of our day says there is no big map, no overarching story, no drama into which we are all swept. There is no story out there we can all trust to give us the outline of what is true and meaningful and good. We are told there is no story big enough and compelling enough to attract us and cause us to attach our own little stories to a bigger, more promising drama. There is no overarching story for our time, no metanarrative, as contemporary philosophers call it. And there is, of course, no one—no authority—designated and trusted to outline the contours of the larger map.

Ultimately we also can read everything in terms that are purely individual. Everything is personal. Everything depends on each of us as individuals, first to deconstruct any meta-map we have been given and then to construct our own separate map. We find ourselves making our own choices about what is meaningful, what is true and good, what is right and wrong, even what is beautiful. This map-making business is up to each of us.

This is the culture in which we live, this world of colliding maps, and the implications for our discussion about higher education and the Christian university are profound. We must ask what our education is like—indeed, what our future will be like—if the very story we pass on to the next generation is a story of no-story or a story of colliding stories. What happens when our definition of human flourishing can be found only in the collision of meanings? What happens as we try to educate in a world of colliding maps?

Hunter has written a disturbing book about how impossible it is to educate for character formation in a world of colliding maps. In this book, titled *The Death of Character: Moral Education in an Age Without Good or Evil*, he argues that there are "structural and cultural realities of our society in this historical moment that make us doubt any kind of transcending narrative."[2] He goes on to say that, without such a larger narrative, there is no chance of teaching character to the next generation, for

> implicit in the word "character" is a story. It is a story about living for a purpose that is greater than the self. . . . The narrative integrates the self within communal purposes binding dissimilar others to common ends. Character outside of a lived community, the entanglements of complex social relationships, and their shared story, is impossible.[3]

And so education is always about telling such a story for our students and for our culture. This is the way we form character through education. But we are trying to do our work in a day and age when any sort of "transcending narrative" is absent. This is one of the reasons, of course, that our universities have virtually abandoned the project of character formation, as my audience in Seattle seemed to argue.

The great theologian, philosopher and missiologist Lesslie Newbigin, echoing the philosopher of science Michael Polanyi, argues that the very act of "knowing is always part of tradition. The mental activity involved in trying to make reliable contact with reality can function only by *indwelling a tradition* of language, concepts, models, images, and assumptions of many kinds which function as the lenses through which we try to find what is really there."[4] In other words, even in the act of trying to know something or trying to teach something, we must see things through the lens of a certain tradition.

Of course, if a culture is going to cohere, there must be some agreement about what tradition we are talking about, and there must be some level of trust in that tradition. Otherwise it is impossible for knowledge to be discovered, sustained, passed on and renewed from one generation to the next. There must always be a story through which we seek to understand the world, and education historically is about telling that story.

---

[2]James Davison Hunter, *The Death of Character: Moral Education in an Age Without Good or Evil* (New York: Basic Books, 2000), p. xiii.
[3]Ibid., pp. 226-27.
[4]Lesslie Newbigin, *Proper Confidence: Faith, Doubt, and Certainty in Christian Discipleship* (Grand Rapids: Eerdmans, 1995), pp. 47-48.

The problem for our postmodern moment is that *the lens itself* has become the main story we are willing to affirm. We are preoccupied, to say the least, with the lens rather than the picture. We are so obsessed with *looking* that we have come to question whether there really is something to look at. All knowledge is contextualized, we now know, by the culture out of which it comes, and it is this contextualizing, the shaping of knowledge by each culture or each person, that has become the focus and attention of postmodern reflection and indeed the business of the university.

It is this floating and bumping and colliding that defines the culture of our postmodern moment. And it is this same free-floating swirl that shapes the contours of a paradigm within which we must do our work as educators.

——————————————————— ▪ ———————————————————

Since the middle of the nineteenth century, intellectuals, writers and philosophers began to form this deep suspicion that there is no overarching narrative of meaning. We find this suspicion supremely in Nietzsche, of course, and we find it in almost all the important literary voices of the late nineteenth century and the early twentieth century. Newbigin traced it all the way back to Descartes in the seventeenth century, that pivotal philosopher who declared that the very process of thinking is the source of our very existence, the only certainty about which we can be certain. From there we have taken any number of steps to say finally that it is the thinking subject that is responsible for drawing up our own little maps.

An oft-quoted passage from William Butler Yeats's 1921 poem "Second Coming" captures the early-twentieth-century anxiety about this splintering, this terrific sense of things coming apart. In his memorable image of the falcon losing all connection to the falconer, Yeats sketches the consequences, *the feel*, of living in a world of colliding maps:

Turning and turning in the widening gyre
The falcon cannot hear the falconer;
Things fall apart; the centre cannot hold;

Mere anarchy is loosed upon the world,
The blood-dimmed tide is loosed, and everywhere
The ceremony of innocence is drowned;
The best lack all conviction, while the worst
Are full of passionate intensity.

In this vivid image, we get the acute sense of loss of connection. There is nothing left that is powerful enough to draw us to the center. There is no compelling authority that can hold us together; the falconer becomes irrelevant, powerless. We feel the threat that we just might spin out of control. There is no coherence about which we can all agree, and we are floating free from any locus of authority that might determine, guide or inspire our assumptions about what is real and doable.

Is this the way falcons are supposed to act? Have falcons lost all their training and tradition, the habits of their being, so that this chaotic spinning is the nature of their reality? Has anarchy broken loose upon their world? And of course Yeats is not optimistic about what is yet to come out of such loss at the center of culture. He imagines some "rough beast," with a "gaze blank and pitiless as the sun," making its way to the center of our cultural attention. He imagines such a beast, "its hour come round at last," slouching "toward Bethlehem to be born."[5]

Along with Nietzsche, and so many others during this huge transitional moment in culture, having declared that the first coming of the Christ child now no longer holds the attention of the culture from the center, what now is this second coming going to be like? What kind of voice at the center will call us into coherence?

━━━━━━━━━━━━━━━ ∎ ━━━━━━━━━━━━━━━

"Things fall apart; the centre cannot hold"; "anarchy is loosed upon the world"—this is exactly Potok's world of colliding maps.

These describe in part the crisis in education today. Even while we believe we soar fiercely and wildly and beautifully, there is yet a yearning here for a falconer to call us to a center. There must be training and

---

[5]William Butler Yeats, "The Second Coming," in *Selected Poems and Two Plays of William Butler Yeats*, ed. M. L. Rosenthal (New York: Collier Books, 1962), p. 91.

tradition for the falcon to fly so beautifully. Education can take place only within a given and coherent tradition, and some kind of authority is essential if that tradition is to be trusted.

Hannah Arendt, that wonderfully insightful mid-twentieth century philosopher, says that "authority has vanished from the modern world," and we have experienced "the loss of worldly permanence and reliability." Further, "the whole dimension of the past has also been endangered. We are in danger of forgetting" and such "oblivion" means we will lose the "dimension of depth in human existence."[6] How can we imagine a credible educational process in such a world? We must ask for *something more.*

---

[6]Hannah Arendt, *Between Past and Future: Eight Exercises in Political Thought* (New York: Penguin Books, 1961), pp. 91-95.

4

WHAT HAPPENS WHEN WE SIMPLY DON'T KNOW WHAT TO SAY?

Maybe the simple truth is that adult institutions no longer try to talk about character and virtue because they simply wouldn't know what to say.

DAVID BROOKS

We want decency without the authority to insist upon it; we want moral community without any limitations to personal freedom. In short we want what we cannot possibly have on the terms that we want it.

JAMES DAVISON HUNTER

Education . . . is where we decide whether we love our children enough not to expel them from our world and leave them to their own devices, nor to strike from their hands their chance of undertaking something new, something unforeseen by us, but to prepare them in advance for the task of renewing a common world.

HANNAH ARENDT

IN HIS LENGTHY STUDY ABOUT STUDENTS at Princeton University, David Brooks says, "Today's students do not inherit a concrete and articulated moral system."[1] Such a system, a guiding narrative, is simply not part of their experience coming into college. I believe Brooks is right, though I remain convinced that students may come to the university seeking such a system. So here is the question: What happens if the university simply goes silent? What happens if it has nothing to say about things that really matter in students' lives?

When I was a young professor, we assumed that students arrived on our campuses as freshmen with a coherent view of the world. While we thought it was a defective view of the world—characterized by the distortions of black-and-white rigidity—at least they brought with them some notion of what is true and good and beautiful. As faculty we believed that our highest responsibility was to shake these students to the core so that they would be disabused of narrowness and dogmatism. At the faculty lunch table, we would ridicule the sorry state of our naïve incoming students in so many eloquent and witty ways. Just wait until they hit our classes. We would force them to move through the sometimes painful process of liberation from dogmatism. We were thrilled to inflict such pain, because we were convinced it would lead our students to a more generous and nuanced view of the world.

We regarded it as our responsibility, a high calling indeed, to infuse shades of gray into our students' black-and-white outlook. Ambiguity was the name of the game in those days; we believed we needed to teach them to tolerate and even revel in ambiguity. We needed to introduce them to thinking and reading that would lift them out of their simple and limited ways. We would often discuss how best to *jolt* them with a good dose of cognitive dissonance. This was for their own good, of course.

If our students survived this jolting process and stayed with us, we would come alongside to try to help put the pieces back together. Under this developmental paradigm we crafted a passion for ambiguity rather than certainty, suspicion for authority rather than trust. We were de-

---

[1]David Brooks, "The Organization Kid," *The Atlantic*, April 2001, p. 40.

constructing worldviews rather than building up coherent stories about human life and the human community.

Joseph Heller published the novel *Something Happened* at just this time. Suddenly we looked around and saw that, indeed, *something had happened*. Somewhere along the line, educators and scholars became convinced that shades of gray and the fierce promulgation of ambiguity might be a better story than any truth we could teach. Somewhere we decided we really didn't believe in a coherent worldview, even a nuanced and sophisticated one, with which we could put the pieces back together for our students. We sat around examining a "heap of broken images," as T. S. Eliot called it in the early twentieth century.[2] At some point, people in the university started putting quotation marks around the word *truth*. Something happened. Something changed.

Alarmingly, the university does not have, Brooks says, "a set of ideals to instruct [these] privileged men and women on how to live, how to see their duties, and how to call upon their highest efforts."[3] There used to be a common story. But the common story went away, and the academy did its best to banish it. Brooks writes,

> Although today's Princeton and today's parents impose all sorts of rules to reduce safety risks and encourage achievement, they do not go to great lengths to build character, the way adults and adult institutions did a century ago. They don't offer much help with the fundamental questions.

And why not? Brooks quotes a Princeton dean: Because "[we made] the decision that these are adults and this is not our job." Brooks continues, "When it comes to character and virtue, these young people have been left on their own . . . go figure out what is true and just for yourselves."[4]

In other words, you are on your own to draw your own map about how to live, by what standards, values and virtues you will make your choices. You are on your own to sketch out a vision for a better world.

---

[2]T. S. Eliot, "The Waste Land," in *The Waste Land and Other Poems* (New York: Harcourt, Brace & World, 1930), p. 30.
[3]David Brooks, "The Organization Kid."
[4]Ibid.

We will provide the skills for you to operate at the highest levels of our society, but we will not give you the map of meaning by which you might effectively use those competencies. According to Brooks,

> We assume that each person has to solve these questions alone (though few other societies in history have made this assumption). We assume that if adults try to offer moral instruction, it will just backfire, because our children will reject our sermonizing (though they don't seem to reject any other part of our guidance and instruction). We assume that such questions have no correct answer that can be taught.

And here is the punch line: "Maybe the simple truth is that adult institutions no longer try to talk about character and virtue because they simply wouldn't know what to say," says Brooks.[5]

Rather than welcoming our incoming students into a world of coherence and meaning, can it be that we have very little to say about matters of ultimate importance, things like the formation of character or the shaping of a moral universe by which to make life's critical choices? Perhaps the university has decided it has no framework from which to provide our students guidance as they make choices about relationships or sexuality or marriage or health, or as they make ethical decisions in business or the professions.

Hunter says, "Character matters, we believe, because without it, trust, justice, freedom, community, and stability are probably impossible."[6] Character matters, indeed. We see the consequences of its absence all around us, from corruption and dishonesty within our corporations, to plagiarism among historians, to falsified data among scientists, to pilots getting on commercial airplanes drunk, to financiers building massive schemes that collapse like a house of cards. Character matters big-time. Our very lives depend on it.

But Hunter says quite bluntly that "character is dead. Attempts to revive it will yield little. Its time has passed. . . . The social and cultural conditions that make character possible are no longer present and no amount of political rhetoric, legal maneuvering, educational policy

---

[5]Ibid.
[6]James Davison Hunter, *The Death of Character: Moral Education in an Age Without Good or Evil* (New York: Basic Books, 2000), p. 6.

making, or money can change that reality. Its time has passed."[7]

Character is dead because there is no unifying story, no credible, common set of values within the culture, to provide the foundations of what character is and how it should be formed. "We Americans see all around us," Hunter says, "the fragmentation of our public life, our increasing inability to speak to each other through a common moral vocabulary."[8] Within such a culture, it is impossible to teach character—though, ironically, we may claim the great importance of character for the health of our society and the future of our world. "We say we want a renewal of character in our day," says Hunter, "but we don't really know what we ask for. To have a renewal of character is to have a renewal of a creedal order that constrains, limits, binds, obligates, and compels. This price is too high for us to pay."[9]

The university of our day is not about to place itself within the boundaries of any kind of "creedal order," any story, any tradition that binds or obligates or compels. That, of course, would be to acknowledge a truth claim, and truth claims are only for the private domain and must never be allowed to hold sway in public. Truth claims would constrain our vaunted notion of freedom—academic, social and personal freedom. We don't want anything constraining or limiting any part of our prized freedom.

When we create a social order where there is nothing to set boundaries, no constraints, no limits or obligations, no authority, no map to guide the way, we think we have created a truly free community. But are we really set free?

"We want decency without the authority to insist upon it," Hunter says. "We want moral community without any limitations to personal freedom. In short we want what we cannot possibly have on the terms that we want it."[10] We may regret from time to time that we are floating on maps of our own constructing, and that we are thereby precluded from teaching character, but we really don't want it any other way.

---

[7]Ibid., p. xiii.
[8]Ibid., p. 9.
[9]Ibid., p. xv.
[10]Ibid.

Arendt makes a very touching statement about our responsibilities toward the young people we have the privilege to educate:

> Education is the point at which we decide whether we love the world enough to assume responsibility for it and by the same token save it from that ruin which, except for renewal, except for the coming of the new and young, would be inevitable. And education, too, is where we decide whether we love our children enough not to expel them from our world and leave them to their own devices, nor to strike from their hands their chance of undertaking something new, something unforeseen by us, but to prepare them in advance for the task of renewing a common world.[11]

An education that abrogates, neglects and even denies the existence of a common story through which we might pass on a vision for human flourishing is an education devoid of love in the end—love for our world and love for our children. We must do better than this. But we must go about the hard work of imagining and constructing an alternative. This is where the Christian university, rightly focused and at its best, enters the picture.

---

[11]Hannah Arendt, *Between Past and Future: Eight Exercises in Political Thought* (New York: Penguin Books, 1961), p. 196.

CAMPUS LIFE WITHOUT
A GUIDING STORY

They find themselves in a world of unprecedented ambiguity,
where it's not clear if you're going out with the person you're
having sex with, where it's not clear if anything
can be said to be absolutely true.

DAVID BROOKS

THE SOMETIMES BRILLIANT, ALWAYS intriguing novelist-journalist
Tom Wolfe has written a sprawling novel about college life in our
time. He gives us a glimpse of what it is like to go to college in a world
of colliding maps. I am talking here about Wolfe's 2004 novel, *I Am
Charlotte Simmons*.

Wolfe's picture of university life has been disputed by some as sensa-
tional and exaggerated, and it has been generally ignored by the press
and defensively disregarded by most of higher education. But it provides the brutal honesty we need when talking about a campus life
unhooked from a guiding story of what is true and good and beautiful.
If every parent of every child going to college was required to read this
novel before the beginning of school, we might at the least spark some
stimulating discussion about the deeper purpose of the university.
Something is missing in the college world of Charlotte Simmons,
something vital, something profoundly important to any healthy notion of education.

■

I Am Charlotte Simmons follows the main character as she makes her way from a rural town through her freshman year on the quintessential big university campus, the fictional Dupont University. Dupont is full of all the intrigue, the delights and the absurdities of university life. This includes the enormous power the basketball coach has over the university president. We witness as well the pretense of faculty influence, the outright silliness of political correctness and the sometimes raw underside of fraternity culture gone wild.

Charlotte finds herself "feeling quite intellectual" one morning on her way to class. She encounters there her brilliant, peripatetic professor, one Victor Ransome Starling. She is "transported," enraptured by the thrill of it all. There was "something ineffably noble and majestic" about the way Professor Starling opened up new worlds of understanding, pacing the stage with such poise. He could offer up such outbursts of brilliance, exposing angles on life and history and discovery Charlotte could not have dreamed possible just months ago before arriving on campus. Here we find that lovely freshman encounter with the joy of learning—the romance of learning, as Alfred North Whitehead called this developmental stage. Oh the joy of it all: Professor Starling "would lead her," she felt confident on that morning, "to the innermost secrets of life."[1]

Charlotte comes to this classroom with openness, trust and eagerness, sitting there enraptured, ready to be shaped, vulnerable in her openness. And how will this professor handle this precious gift of trust and eagerness she has given him? Is the purpose of the university structured in such a way to honor this gift of trust she has laid so bare and so honestly? When given this extraordinary opportunity, will the university give her bread instead of a stone?

We begin to get the answer to these questions. One side sermon Professor Starling indulges in that morning is that the "denigration of another culture, especially one whose people are less well off than your own, and referring to anything as evil, which would indicate you might

---

[1]Tom Wolfe, *I Am Charlotte Simmons* (New York: Farrar, Straus, Giroux, 2004), p. 390.

very well have religious convictions, were more socially unacceptable at Dupont" than anything else.[2] The highest virtue of the university is to affirm any cultural map, any person's map, as long as that map is intelligent, clever and clear, *and* as long as that map does not venture close to anything like the truth claims of religion. "And people don't call anything evil," the professor admonishes his class that morning.

But the real lecture of the morning was about the "first giant of modern neuroscience," Jose Delgado, who placed himself in front of a raging bull, only to zap an electrode that had been inserted in the bull's brain. This scientist stood there calm and confident that this manipulation would turn the bull from rage to a loping and demurring beast, just before impact.

Young, bright and eager, Charlotte was beginning to get the point, that "we are the product of external forces."[3] Marx and Freud both demonstrated this, says her adored professor, but Marx and Freud are "sheer whimsy compared to that of the neuroscientist." This is philosophical materialism at its best. Here then we locate another piece of the orthodoxy of the university of our day. Anything we might call spiritual is an illusion. It is nonexistent.

And so the university begins to unfold its intellectual framework to the open, eager and trusting Charlotte. But finally such intellectual explorations and discoveries are overwhelmed by the strong, raw and relentless forces of social acceptance and peer negotiations. Really at the bottom of it all, or in addition to the intellectual formation she seeks, Charlotte comes to Dupont expecting to find a caring and nurturing community.

Once again she comes with that utterly innocent posture of trust. Is it too much for a freshman to ask that the university keep her safe to grow and test and mature?

What Charlotte finds is a dog-eat-dog world of adolescence, a community of colliding social and moral maps. She is absolutely and profoundly floating about on her own. She understands quickly that the student world is fundamentally and intentionally cut from any oversight

[2]Ibid., p. 391.
[3]Ibid., p. 393.

or guidance. There are no adults in sight to help point the way. She discovers at Dupont no intentional community in which she can find boundaries of what is acceptable, appropriate and decent. There will be no loving arms of support and encouragement when the going inevitably gets tough for a young person suddenly on her own in college.

Charlotte goes to the spring dance of the most popular fraternity with what is apparently one of the popular guys. This is a kind of badge of acceptance she longs for. She wants to have fun, to be sure, but she wants also to be accepted, to be cool, to find community. After a lot of alcohol and a lot of raucous dancing and bantering, most of it fashioned by the standards of young males, Charlotte is led, dazed by drink and bedazzled by the prospect of finally being accepted, perhaps even loved, into the real secrets of life on the campus of Dupont: "She was excited, a bit frightened, but more than anything else curious. What exactly would he do now?" "Was this what men did?" she kept asking herself.

And she gets her answer as she is led, trusting and naive, into a horrifying encounter of date rape. She discovers the utter emptiness and loneliness she so much wanted to escape. Was there no one who might have told her the rules of this game? Was there no one who might have, shall we say, quite traditionally, *protected* her from this damaging encounter? Is this really the territory the university should keep its hands off?

She discovers out of painful experience that there is simply no intimacy to be found at this party. After being forcefully raped, all the while wondering if this is what men do, toward the end trying to resist, sometimes enticed and excited, sometimes naively enticing and encouraging, when it was all over "she curled herself up into a ball. She took a self-destructive, self-hating pleasure" in looking at herself as "a little fool but also to a little fool's illusion that men fell in love. Men didn't *fall* in love, which would be surrender. They *made* love—*made* being an active, transitive verb that rhymed with *raid*, the marauder out for blood . . ."[4]

---

[4]Ibid., p. 469.

And here we come full circle with a campus culture unwilling to call anything wrong, a university with its soul hollowed out. Here we find the personal end to the road of an intellectual construct that deems all cultures acceptable, all sense of the self mechanical and material, notions of right and wrong beyond the appropriate purview of judgment. These young men, and their sometimes-willing female companions, get the message of a world of colliding maps: You are on your own; make of it whatever you please; in fact, draw up your map according to what pleases you most; there are no boundaries; there is no story to guide you; and there are certainly no adults around to point the way.

In one of his columns in the *New York Times*, David Brooks says of Wolfe's novel that

> he's located one of the paradoxes of the age. Highly educated young people are tutored, taught and monitored in all aspects of their lives, except the most important, which is character building. When it comes to this, most universities leave them alone. And they find themselves in a world of *unprecedented ambiguity*, where it's not clear if you're going out with the person you're having sex with, where it's not clear if anything can be said to be absolutely true.[5]

———————————— ■ ————————————

In an article in *Christianity Today* called "Dorm Brothel: The New Debauchery, and the Colleges That Let It Happen," Vigen Guroian confesses his dismay at the world we have constructed on our university campuses. Guroian, a professor of theology at Loyola College in Baltimore, says, "As a college professor and father of a college-age daughter . . . I am outraged by the complicity of my college and most other schools in the death of courtship and the emergence of a dangerous and destructive culture of 'hooking up.'"[6] This is what Charlotte Simmons wonders about as well, this phenomenon of hooking up. Was she really

[5]David Brooks, "Moral Suicide a la Wolfe," *New York Times*, November 16, 2004, sec. A27 (emphasis added).
[6]Vigen Guroian, "Dorm Brothel: The New Debauchery, and the Colleges That Let It Happen," *Christianity Today*, February 2005, p. 23.

"hooking up?" she asks. "So now she'd really done it, hooked up."[7]

And just what is hooking up? "'Hooking up' is dating," says Guroian, "*sans* courtship or expectations of a future relationship or commitment. It is strictly about user sex. I use you and you use me for mutual pleasure. And liquor is more often than not the lubricant that makes things go."[8] Guroian goes on to say that, "in most American college coed dorms, the flesh of our daughters is being served up daily like snack jerky. No longer need young men be wolves or foxes to consume that flesh. There are no fences to jump or chicken coops to break into. The gates are wide open and no guard dogs have been posted. It is easy come and easy go."

He adds, "The sex carnival that is college life today is also doing great damage to our sons' characters, deforming their attitudes toward the opposite sex. I am witnessing a perceptible dissipation of manly virtue in the young men I teach."[9]

Here finally is the point I want to emphasize: "My outcry," says Guroian, "is not directed at the debauchery among college students, but rather at the colleges themselves. They are the wink and nod our colleges give to fornication and dissipation." I am sure this language sounds old and dated and oh-so-very traditional to those who define and defend student life on our college campuses today. It sounds so judgmental, one of the cardinal sins of university life. But this is an "unhealthy and morally destructive environment" we have created in our universities, says Guroian. This is "the grisly underbelly of the modern American college; the deep, dark, hidden secret that many parents suspect is there but would rather not face."[10]

Can this really be one of the untold stories of our university today, a story that has emerged out of this culture of colliding maps? Surely we must be hard at work to imagine and construct an alternative to all this.

---

[7] Wolfe, *I Am Charlotte Simmons*, p. 477.
[8] Guroian, "Dorm Brothel."
[9] Ibid.
[10] Ibid.

THE RED T-SHIRT AND THE
DINNER-TABLE DRAMA

We are a people who know what it is to cross the Red Sea on dry land,
to be fed with manna in the wilderness,
to return with singing from Babylon, to stand before the cross,
and to meet the risen Lord in the breaking of bread.
This is our story, and it defines who we are.

LESSLIE NEWBIGIN

A morally significant universe has a telos, an end, goal, and standard,
by which one knows where one is and to where one is headed.
It thus provides individuals the big script of a very real drama,
in the sense both that the story is intensely dramatic
and that the drama is reality.

CHRISTIAN SMITH

LITERARY THEORIST AND LEGAL SCHOLAR Stanley Fish says that liberalism, that form of rationality shaped by the eighteenth-century Enlightenment,

> rests on the substantive judgment that the public sphere must be insulated
> from viewpoints that owe their allegiance not to its procedures—to the
> unfettered operation of the marketplace of ideas—but to the truths they
> work to establish. That is what neutrality means in the context of liberal-

ism—a continual pushing away of orthodoxies, of beliefs not open to inquiry and correction—and that is why, in the name of neutrality, religious propositions must . . . be excluded from the marketplace.[1]

Fish articulates here, and in so many other places, a *new orthodoxy* for our culture. Our culture is focused precisely on this "continual pushing away" of all ancient orthodoxies. But we must recognize that "the unfettered operation of the marketplace of ideas," that noble purpose of the university since the seventeenth century, took place squarely in the very context of "viewpoints that owe their allegiance" to the "truth they work to establish." "Truth" continued to matter on into the nineteenth century. This is what academic freedom used to mean: unfettered freedom, exuberant and courageous discussion and debate—but all within the framework of an overarching narrative of meaning, a narrative that provided common ground for what we used to call "the pursuit of truth."

But the new orthodoxy becomes the unfettered operation itself. The "marketplace of ideas" is accompanied by fierce resistance to frame the discussion with any guiding, overarching narrative. This "neutrality" is the main presupposition itself. And we are told we must be deeply worried about an "allegiance" of any kind, any sort of embrace of anything we regard as true. There must be "a continual pushing away of orthodoxies," especially any "religious propositions."

Theologian Lesslie Newbigin says that such claims for neutrality are "evidence either of impending collapse or else of the fact that some other ideology has taken the place usually occupied by religion."[2] Either we are anticipating the collapse of the culture, where nothing matters on the things that matter, where unfettered freedom without regard to substance reigns; *or* we are in the middle of ideological battles that seek to fill the vacuum left by the departure of religion. Here we find a prevalent and prevailing nihilism projected by Nietzsche at the end of the nineteenth century.

Surely we must do better than this. As Newbigin reminds us, "total skepticism about ultimate beliefs is strictly impossible." The kind of

---

[1]Stanley Fish, "Why We Can't All Just Get Along," *First Things* 60 (February 1996): 18-26.
[2]Lesslie Newbigin, *Foolishness to the Greeks: The Gospel and Western Culture* (Grand Rapids: Eerdmans, 1986), p. 138.

philosophical neutrality Fish promotes is "always in danger of giving place to some sort of fanaticism that can be as intolerant as any religion has ever been."[3] We must choose our "orthodoxies" carefully and well. But as we sit here in "the midst of a plurality of worlds," as Newbigin notes, what are our choices? If we must decide on the map that will guide our way, how do we do it? I am convinced we must first recognize fully that this plurality of choices is the cultural reality of our day. If this is so, then we must find a way to understand, embrace and articulate a compelling narrative of what is true and good and beautiful. We must choose our map and ride it confidently.

Let me introduce two new metaphors into our discussion. The first comes from an experience I had a few years ago while I was boarding a plane. I was fumbling with my papers and books, and trying to take my seat in the oh-so-crowded space, when I suddenly noticed a college-age woman coming down the aisle wearing a red T-shirt. I was stunned into reflection when I read the message emblazoned across the front: "DENY EVERYTHING." Let us assume that this was the story she had emphatically chosen for herself. This was not, to be sure, a grand claim to remain blissfully neutral. She was taking a stand, choosing her story. She was sketching out her map, and her story was emphatically to deny the claims of all stories. While claiming to deny everything, of course, she was making a truth claim that she had the right and the ability to do such denying—but this was the story, the truth claim, that would apparently anchor her life.

This young woman would agree with our most sophisticated postmodernist understanding of human communication that created texts of our culture, written texts of any sort, must be treated with utmost suspicion. She would agree that she must deny what every text *seems* to be saying, because it must be saying something beyond or beneath what it says. Something beneath the surface wants to abuse and hold power

---

[3]Ibid.

over her. That something wants to violate her sense of inviolable freedom and independence. We call this mindset the *hermeneutic of suspicion*, one of the hallmarks of the contemporary university, one of the resonant strategies of postmodernism. No text has any right to speak with authority, and all texts are somehow deceiving, even self-deceiving. And so our young woman must be vigilant in her denial of all things written and communicated.

The sad part of this little emblem, this red T-shirt, is that this young woman is very likely learning to sketch out such a life within the halls of our colleges and universities. She is absorbing this map through pop culture, media and entertainment, perhaps as well from her family, but her university represents those various cultures in a way that is respectable, convincing and compelling to her. I cannot help but suspect that this young woman with the red T-shirt arrived at college one fine September morning with fresh expectations, an innocence, a trust and an eagerness, just as the fictional Charlotte Simmons embarked on her college career at the prestigious Dupont University.

Deny everything! This is a story that speaks of courage, independence and personal authority. It says that I can simplify the sometimes overwhelming confusion of the competing stories swirling around. I can perhaps tame what the British novelist Ian McEwan called the "unbearable complexity" of our time. Perhaps this is a story—this need to deny everything—that comes out of betrayal, abuse and broken trust. Perhaps it is a story that comes out of the profound absence of adults, people in her life who might assume responsibility to help define the world and to teach with authority. No need to debate, in this world, just deny. No need to make a case that is convincing or compelling, just deny. No need to risk trust in some authority, only to have that trust broken—just deny them all. No need to gather up all the courage you can muster and trust someone or some view of the world. Just deny.

In *Veritatis Splendor*, Pope John Paul II calls this tendency toward denial a "crisis of truth" in our time. He says that "certain currents of modern thought have gone so far as to exalt freedom to such an extent that it becomes an absolute, which would then be the source of values."[4] In other words, this utterly individualistic posture of denying everything is the only absolute. It is from that perch that we become the final authority on all questions, indeed the authoritative "source of values."

The Pope goes further to lay responsibility even at the feet of theologians in the church, where this direction is "taken by doctrines which have lost the sense of the transcendent."[5] With no transcendent dimension, in other words, it is up to each individual to be the final authority, the absolute determinant, in matters of meaning and purpose and destiny.

Indeed, if we have eliminated any big story or drama that gives shape, direction and meaning, any notion of the transcendent, "the individual conscience is accorded the status of a supreme tribunal of moral judgment which hands down categorical and infallible decisions about good and evil," John Paul II says. Infallible decisions, but for ourselves alone. If this story wins out, the story in which everything is denied but my own ability and right to deny, "the inescapable claims of truth disappear, yielding their place to a criterion of sincerity, authenticity and 'being at peace with oneself.'"[6] In profound contrast, John Paul II vigorously proposed an embrace, through courageous faith, of the "splendor of truth."

I will have more to say on the splendor of truth later, but first let's think about another metaphor, another way of imagining a guiding story for our lives. My father died a few years ago, and in the midst of grieving and remembering, I reflected on what sort of legacy he handed down to me. My reflections came into focus around the evenings we spent at the family dinner table of my childhood. Though I am sure I look back now with a kind of idealizing glow, I do believe this table was blessed.

First, this table was touched by the gift of my mother's artistry: good and plentiful food. This was an expression of her beautiful sense of

---

[4]Pope John Paul II, *"Veritatis Splendor* (The Splendor of Truth)," Encyclical Letter, 1993.
[5]Ibid.
[6]Ibid.

calling, an enormous contribution to the possibilities of family. The table was also blessed by the force of my father's belief that life was a big unfolding drama. And so there we were, sitting around that table, my brothers and sister, my parents and me, most certainly an insignificant little group, but nevertheless caught up in the flow of a big drama that was far bigger than our little table.

We would talk about politics and culture and war and foreign lands, all of which were mysterious to a young boy—complex, threatening at times, exciting, alluring. We would talk about people, leaders who deserved our respect and even adoration, but also of pastors, evangelists and politicians who had fallen because of sex or money. We talked about men and women who were doing heroic things; we made room for heroes at the table, for models.

In all of this conversation and storytelling, we got the picture that there was a big drama going on out there, and we were encouraged to pay attention, ultimately to find our place and to play our part. We were encouraged to *engage* in that drama. There was no room for separatism or isolation at this little dinner table. We had no inkling, no illusion, that we were the sole creators of this story, the only and final authority, the final source of values, meaning, direction and purpose.

And then an amazing thing happened each evening at our little table. After we had finished our meal, my father would reach for the Bible at the stand beside the table. Now, I confess that I was ready at this point, like any young kid, to head out to play with my friends before dark. But my father's voice took control, and we understood clearly that we were entering into something we should not violate. His voice would change somehow, grow reverent, deeper, resonant. We knew we were stepping into holy space, a world of rich and mysterious stories, a world of beautiful and nuanced language, a world that had direction and purpose, a world where every event, every word, seemed loaded with meaning. We also sensed we were stepping into a world full of promise and hope. We knew there must be something true and good about this bigger, amazing story.

We stepped into that world each evening with awe and curiosity, baffled at times, encouraged at times, chastised and challenged. But in hindsight we knew we had been handed the animating center of the stories we told around our little table. We knew our little stories were swept up in a really big, unfolding drama. In Jürgen Moltmann's words, we somehow knew that "the glow that suffuses everything here is the dawn of an expected new day."[7] The big unfolding drama of the Scriptures, so mysterious at times and yet so compelling, told us vividly to expect that new day.

We became aware, as Lesslie Newbigin clearly states, that "we are a people who know what it is to cross the Red Sea on dry land, to be fed with manna in the wilderness, to return with singing from Babylon, to stand before the cross, and to meet the risen Lord in the breaking of bread. This is our story, and it defines who we are."[8] We are all asking the question, says Newbigin, "Who am I?" and "What is my story?" In other words, what is the story by which I will live and make choices? And the further question we asked at our little dinner table is, as Newbigin asks, "What is the whole story of which my story is a part?" We somehow could see quite clearly, as my father reached for the holy text, that "to indwell the Bible is to live with an answer to those questions."[9]

At just about the time I was encountering this huge and meaningful drama at the dinner table of my childhood, the political theorist Hannah Arendt was sizing up the implications of a world without such overarching drama. In 1961, even before the postmodern attack on the notion of a metanarrative began in earnest, she said, "We have ceased to live in a common world where the words we have in common possess an unquestionable meaningfulness."

This is frightening. This is what happens when we live in a world of colliding maps. This is what happens when we deny everything and so anoint ourselves as the final arbiter of meaning, value, purpose and even language. The results are not pretty, says Arendt, because "short of being condemned to live verbally in an altogether meaningless world, we grant each other the right to retreat into our own worlds of mean-

---

[7]Jürgen Moltmann, *Theology of Hope: On the Ground and the Implications of a Christian Eschatology* (1967; reprint, Minneapolis: Fortress, 1993), p. 16.
[8]Lesslie Newbigin, *The Gospel in a Pluralist Society* (Grand Rapids: Eerdmans, 1989), p. 100.
[9]Ibid., p. 110.

ing, and demand only that each of us remain consistent within his own private terminology."[10]

This is what happens when we speak utterly different languages. We live in cloisters of our own making, retreats of meaning, living in the suffocating space of our "private terminology" alone. This is what happens when unfettered freedom is never challenged by any kind of orthodoxy. This is decidedly not the world of my little dinner table.

——————————————— ■ ———————————————

If we are going to write the story of the American university of our time, which will it be: The story in which we are compelled to deny everything, the story where we are at the center of the universe, the story of profound philosophical neutrality about all stories? Or will it be a story with a big, unfolding drama, a story out there we choose to embrace as true, even with all the complexities of such a claim? Which kind of university do we want as we seek to make the world a better place for all of God's children?

The Christian university I am imagining in these pages *makes a choice*. Even in the face of "a continual pushing away of orthodoxies" so pervasive in our culture, the Christian university chooses an *animating center* to its work as a university. God's drama is the big and profoundly meaningful drama out there. This drama has a beginning and a history, and we live in the middle as the story continues to unfold. Most importantly we are filled with hope and joy because our drama has a future defined by reconciliation, peace, love and flourishing beyond the imagination. The Christian university we are imagining does its work right smack in the midst of the vibrant swirl of this extraordinary drama.

And so we lift up a radical alternative in the world of higher education today, truly another way of educating. And we assert, with some measure of cultural savvy, that this can indeed be the place where world change begins.

---

[10]Hannah Arendt, *Between Past and Future: Eight Exercises in Political Thought* (New York: Penguin Books, 1961), pp. 95-96.

THE PRESUMPTION OF UNBELIEF
AND THE CONSEQUENCES

For you know only
A heap of broken images, where the sun beats,
And the dead tree gives no shelter, the cricket no relief,
And the dry stone no sound of water.

T. S. ELIOT

What did we do when we unchained this earth from its sun?
Whither is it moving now? Whither are we moving now? Away from
all suns? Are we not plunging continually? Backward, sideward,
forward, in all directions? Is there any up or down left?
Are we not straying as through an infinite nothing?

FRIEDRICH NIETZSCHE

STANLEY FISH ARTICULATES SO WELL AND in so many places the underlying presuppositions of our profoundly and pervasively secular society. We are shaped, and by implication the secular university is shaped, by "the modern liberal-enlightenment picture of cognitive activity," he says. Here our work is framed by a strategy "in which the mind is conceived of as a calculating and assessing machine that is open to all thoughts and closed to none. In this picture the mind is in an important sense not yet settled; and indeed settling, in the form of a fixed commitment to an idea or a value, is a sign of cognitive and moral infirmity."[1] This is as clear a picture as any to define the starting point, the orthodoxy, that lies at the heart of our secular culture.

If this is a guiding story for our culture, and for the university that both reflects and supports that culture, there seems to be a fundamental tension right at the center of such a position. What if an individual has indeed "settled," through an act of courageous faith, that Jesus Christ is Lord over all of life? Despite the assertion of total freedom of thought, such a claim about Jesus, made in private, apparently is not welcome at the table of discourse and debate, what we sometimes call the public square. And so we are not really "open to all thoughts and closed to none." Of course, this notion drives that ever-prevalent bifurcation in modern culture that relegates "matters of belief" to the private sphere, while what we believe to be "matters of fact" are for the more important public arena.

Fish, by the way, always reveals his bias in the nuances of his language, elegant as it always is. In this case he labels any commitment in faith as "settled" and "fixed," as if one cannot embrace a particular story of what is true and at the same time live out a vibrant life of faith that is always changing and maturing. How absurd to create such a static caricature of Christian commitment, a notion that is theologically unsound for most Christians.

The main point Fish is making is that we are supposed to be "open to all thoughts and closed to none." We prize that freedom, what we used to call the pursuit of truth. This is what we laud as academic freedom. The university would not be what it is without this abiding commitment to radical openness. The Christian university has no problem with this openness, despite rumors to the contrary. And yet for our culture, and I suspect for much of the modern university, any idea that is "settled," affirmed by faith and trust to be true, must be denied as "moral infirmity." In this view, any embrace of faith is both belittled and dismissed as a legitimate source of understanding and wisdom.

How did we get to this place? And what are the consequences for our lives, for our society and for our universities? In his important work on

---

[1]Stanley Fish, "Why We Can't All Just Get Along," *First Things* 60 (February 1996): 19.

the dramatic cultural shift from a "background" of belief to a "background" of choice about belief, the philosopher and historian Charles Taylor calls this shift "a titanic change in our western civilization."[2] James Davison Hunter calls it "mind-boggling." He says,

> At the time that John Locke died and Rousseau was born in the early years of the eighteenth century, it was unimaginable that the authority of Christendom would ever be diminished. Its institutions and its authority were unassailable. Yet in less than a century, traditional Christian authority and the regime it spawned and maintained had either been overturned (as in France) or had been forever weakened. In this we see a cultural transformation of world historical significance.[3]

In Taylor's 2007 book *A Secular Age*, he traces the contours and nuances of this deep and permanent shift of culture. He says that we moved "from a society in which it was virtually impossible not to believe in God, to one in which faith, even for the staunchest believer, is one human possibility among others."[4] This is where the world became a world of colliding maps, a world where settling into belief is too often regarded as "a sign of cognitive and moral infirmity."

Taylor talks about the university in the context of such a secular age. He says, "Our modern civilization is made up of a host of societies, subsocieties and milieu, all rather different from each other." As we have seen, this very "host of societies" has no overarching story that brings congruence to the myriad options available. But "the presumption of unbelief has become dominant in more and more of these milieu; and has achieved hegemony in certain crucial ones, in academic and intellectual life, for instance; whence it can more easily extend itself to others."[5] Notice here that Taylor still assumes the influence of the university, which extends this dominant "presumption of unbelief" out to other parts of our society. The university remains most surely a force in shaping our culture.

[2]Charles Taylor, *A Secular Age* (Cambridge, Mass.: Belknap Press of Harvard University Press, 2007), p. 12.
[3]James Davison Hunter, *To Change the World: The Irony, Tragedy, and Possibility of Christianity in the Late Modern World* (New York: Oxford University Press, 2010), p. 75.
[4]Taylor, *A Secular Age*, p. 3.
[5]Ibid., pp. 12-13.

We live in a world with a "plurality of options." Christians everywhere must accept this as our new context of culture. Pluralism is a fact of our lives, and "belief in God is no longer axiomatic," Taylor says. "There are alternatives. And this will also likely mean that at least in certain milieu, it may be hard to sustain one's faith." He continues, "There will be people who feel bound to give it up, even though they mourn its loss. This has been a recognizable experience in our societies, at least since the mid-nineteenth century. There will be many others to whom faith never even seems an eligible possibility. There are certainly millions today of whom this is true."[6] Perhaps our students come into the university with some notion of faith intact, however inarticulate, and then they experience this "background" of presumed unbelief. And they "feel bound to give up" their faith. Is this really what we want from our universities?

◼

The nineteenth century, and of course much of the twentieth century, can be characterized by what Thomas Cahill calls a "hinge of history." This moment in history is a great turning point, where all kinds of forces press in on a fulcrum, forcing dramatic change in the way things are viewed. We hear in the voice of Western writers throughout this historical moment a tone, a kind of voice of the age, a set of images, all gathering force to give expression to what this new, emerging secular world feels like. If we listen carefully to these writers, we invariably hear a sense of loss, indeed a mourning. We experience through them a sense of vertigo, a loss of direction, a loss of hope. This is a world, in this transition, without joy, without wonderment, often with a profoundly uncertain sense of the future. These are the consequences of the seismic cultural shift to a "presumption of unbelief" in the culture.

So many writers of this time were challenged by deep disappointment that the progress promised by the Enlightenment had not come

---

[6]Ibid., p. 3.

to pass. From the seventeenth century forward, many intellectuals had put their trust in the power and efficacy of reason. They believed that reason, properly used, promised nothing short of utopia, the answer to all human suffering, the path to prosperity. The powerful notion of progress was at the heart of this movement, the notion that any human problem placed under the orderly and progressive scrutiny of reason and science would crack wide open with new possibilities. They were on their way with new hope toward human flourishing and prosperity. This notion settled into Western culture as an unquestioned paradigm, strands of which still inform our understanding of human life and destiny.

What we do not understand now, our Enlightenment sages proposed, will one day be clear, given time and the abiding structures of rational scrutiny. The march of science was exhilarating and heartening. Until this transitional moment, there was no reason to suspect that this new hope was anything but divinely guided. God approved of such progress. This was part of God's plan all along. All was well and getting better. This was an exhilarating moment in the history of education, and universities carried this banner of rational scrutiny and progress. As the university began to shake off the shackles of pre-Enlightenment thinking, including what was perceived more and more as the constraints of religion, the future seemed very bright indeed.

But then things began to unravel. Various writers and intellectuals became acutely aware of the damaging consequences of the Industrial Revolution, for example. Born out of the application of science and reason, this promising revolution began to unleash damage and destruction across the cherished natural landscape. Many writers began to peek behind the veil of industrial progress to witness the scourge of horrific working conditions, especially for women, children and others who were vulnerable.

These writers were devastated by the violent, oppressive outcome of the French Revolution, which had held out such promise for intellectuals all over Europe. In the beginning, the revolution promised that reason, coupled with liberty and empowered by the strong forces of common men and women—the masses—would usher in a new day of individual freedom and prosperity. But by the end of the revolution, after the blood of thousands had been spilled in the streets of Paris, the luster of reason, decisively severed from all despised authority, had lost its shine.

These writers clearly understood as well the cultural implications of the massive paradigm shift in the scientific understanding Darwin initiated. They knew that the powerful expression of his discoveries, exhilarating in its fresh new angles, was a profound challenge to all tradition and authority. Darwin's new paradigm was part of the shifting tectonic plates beneath Western culture during this dramatic moment in history. As these writers came to grasp the power of scientific observation, they also knew that Darwin had at least unleashed the question, both culturally and for individuals, of whether there was a need for God.

It was a time to brood, indeed, a time to reflect, a time of passing, a time of enormous uncertainty. It was a time of profound shifts in notions of God and of the authority and accuracy of the Bible. All philosophical, theological and cultural presuppositions were placed on the table for scrutiny and examination, and the only option was to remain open to enormous change.

The Victorian English poet and critic Matthew Arnold found himself "wandering between two worlds, one dead, / The other powerless to be born."[7] These dramatic shifts were inevitable. Of that our writers were sure. But always, it seems, we hear in their tone, their images and their stories, a recognition that something deep and important was being abandoned, never to be retrieved. And then we hear, over and over, a profound uncertainty about where the world was headed.

■

In 1922, in one of the definitive statements of this transitional moment, T. S. Eliot wrote in *The Waste Land* that we find ourselves sitting on

a heap of broken images, where the sun beats,

---

[7]Matthew Arnold, "Stanzas from the Grande Chartreuse," in *The Norton Anthology of English Literature*, ed. M. H. Abrams et al., 6th ed. (New York: Norton, 1996), p. 2062.

And the dead tree gives no shelter, the cricket no relief,
And the dry stone no sound of water.[8]

The sweeping, coherent Christian story that had informed the culture in the West for so many centuries was now broken apart, tossed into a "heap of broken images." We see fragments of something whole in time past, but now find little nourishment, nothing coherent, no continuity. And as Eliot and so many others looked out across that landscape, now devoid of nourishing roots from which new flowering and flourishing might come, what they saw was the relentless sun beating down and the dry, parched earth unable to bring forth new life.

From an earlier moment in this great transition, we hear something of this same voice in Matthew Arnold's poem "Dover Beach." We listen to Arnold's musings in 1851, the year in which he married the woman with whom he was madly in love. This marriage was made more luscious because it had been resisted by her parents, and we can most certainly sense the fresh hope provided by this new love. But at the same time, we hear his brooding about the direction of the world, once the map of faith had been utterly disconnected from the cultural landscape.

The speaker of the poem stands on the shores of Dover Beach, looking out over the English Channel, glimpsing on "the French coast the light" that "gleams and is gone." He is lulled by the beauty, how "the cliffs of England stand, / Glimmering and vast, out in the tranquil bay." The poet muses:

The sea is calm tonight.
The tide is full, the moon lies fair
Upon the straits. . . .
All seems calm and beautiful and glimmering, and yet,
The Sea of Faith
Was once, too, at the full, and round earth's shore
Lay like the folds of a bright girdle furled.
But now I only hear
Its melancholy, long, withdrawing roar,

---

[8]T. S. Eliot, "The Waste Land," in *The Waste Land and Other Poems* (New York: Harcourt, Brace & World, 1930), p. 30.

Retreating, to the breath
Of the night wind, down the vast edges drear
And naked shingles of the world.
Ah, love, let us be true
To one another! For the world which seems
To lie before us like a land of dreams,
So various, so beautiful, so new,
Hath really neither joy, nor love, nor light
Nor certitude, nor peace, nor help for pain;
And we are here as on a darkling plain
Swept with confused alarms of struggle and flight,
Where ignorant armies clash by night.[9]

This poem is filled with melancholy. The speaker is disturbed, fearful, alarmed by what is happening all over the world. Arnold broods here about the consequences of this remarkable shift, when "the Sea of Faith" has withdrawn, when the "presumption of unbelief" has set in permanently.

What will the consequences be as we live now on "a darkling plain," where there is no tradition and no authority to help make sense of the "confused alarms of struggle and flight, / where ignorant armies clash by night"? And while there is a private joy, where the world seems "to lie before us like a land of dreams, / so various, so beautiful, so new," there seems to be no real connection between this personal meaning and the larger unfolding story of confusion, collision and ignorance.

Arnold captures the tone of loss, defeat and profound discouragement. Where do we go from here? Things seemed so stable and certain, and now we must begin again. There seems no solution but to retreat into our private worlds of meaning, our own little cloisters of seeming certainty. Perhaps love for each other is all we have now, he says, without much assurance. Can we ever think we will change the world for good again? And what might replace this enormous loss of faith that was once "at the full"? What happens now?

---

[9]Matthew Arnold, "Dover Beach," in *The Norton Anthology of English Literature*, ed. M. H. Abrams et al., 6th ed. (New York: Norton, 1996), pp. 2059-60.

•

In 1882 the enormously influential Friedrich Nietzsche pronounced famously that "God is dead." Anyone who claimed to be guided by a notion of God was living an illusion, and to recognize that singular fact was an act of courage. It was Nietzsche's deepest conviction that in European culture, and by extension American culture, God was banished from the human landscape, never to return again. A fabrication of the human imagination in the first place, God was no longer needed.

"This beautiful world history is," Nietzsche says, "a chaotic pile of rubbish." In another place he asks, "Is not night and more night coming on all the while?"[10] In 1865, at the age of twenty-one, Nietzsche wrote to his sister suggesting that it is easy "to accept everything that one has been brought up on and that has gradually struck deep roots," including belief in God. But easy was not the chosen path for Nietzsche, nor was it an honorable one, he thought. Though a much harder road, one must try "to strike new paths, fight the habitual, experiencing the insecurity of independence and the frequent wavering of one's feelings and even one's conscience, proceeding often without any consolation, but ever with the eternal goal of the true, the beautiful, and the good,"[11] at least the way one perceives "the true, the beautiful, and the good" at the moment.

Nietzsche was sketching out his life of individual independence, a deep and profound questioning of all tradition and authority. With all certainty pulled out from under us by the circumstances of history, the advancement of science, the brutality of war and oppression, the only courageous choice is to go our own way. We must question the comfortable path. We must strike out in new, exciting and even frightening directions. Deny everything, because the traditional answers no longer suffice.

"Faith does not offer the least support for a proof of objective truth,"

---

[10]Friedrich Nietzsche, *The Portable Nietzsche*, ed. and trans. Walter Kaufmann (New York: Penguin Books, 1954), p. 95.
[11]Ibid., p. 29.

Nietzsche says early on. "Here the ways of men part: if you wish to strive for peace of soul and pleasure, then believe; if you wish to be a devotee of truth, then inquire."[12] Or "then deny," we might add, without distorting his meaning. Deny everything. Nietzsche fashioned himself to be the "man of renunciation,"[13] the ultimate denier. Elsewhere he announced, "For me the greatest fruitfulness and the greatest enjoyment of existence is: to *live dangerously!* . . . Live at war with your peers and yourselves!"[14] Here we are moving from the presumption of belief to the presumption of unbelief.

A bit later in his life, Nietzsche began to ask the tough questions, such as "What, then, is truth?" While this is the big question of all ages, indeed going back to Pilate's question of Jesus at his trial, it most certainly is the question on the mind of our thinkers and writers at this hinge of history. Truth, said Nietzsche, is "a mobile army of metaphors, metonyms, and anthropomorphisms—in short, a sum of human relations, which have been enhanced, transposed, and embellished poetically and rhetorically, and which after long use seem firm, canonical, and obligatory to a people." This is tradition. This is culture. This is a sense of authority. Resting comfortably and unquestioning in this story is the easy path, and one not acceptable to Nietzsche, because ultimately we discover that "truths are illusions about which one has forgotten that this is what they are; metaphors which are worn out and without sensuous power; coins which have lost their pictures and now matter only as metal, no longer as coins."

"We still do not know where the urge for truth comes from," he continues, "for as yet we have heard only of the obligation imposed by society that it should exist: to be truthful means using the customary metaphors—in moral terms: the obligation to lie according to a fixed convention, to lie herd-like in a style obligatory for all."[15] As we read through Nietzsche, we discover there is nothing more disgusting than to accept the claims of the truth of culture when you know such claims

---

[12]Ibid., p. 30.
[13]Ibid., p. 98.
[14]Ibid., p. 97.
[15]Ibid., pp. 46-47.

are all illusions. There is something in all of this greatly to admire, this courage of independent thinking. Yet there is fear, even horror, at the absence of any guiding drama, any story that can make sense of it all.

The heart of the matter for Nietzsche, the path he ultimately took from which there was no return, was the announcement that "God is dead." Somewhere along the line, according to his argument, the authority of God stood behind the "army of metaphors," even as they were all "embellished poetically and rhetorically." But the metaphors turn out to be an illusion, because there is no authority, no true substance, to back them. When the prop of God is finally pulled out from behind them, the whole thing collapses. And this, of course, is true. This is why our most cherished claims to truth lie in a heap of broken images.

Contemporary philosopher Alasdair MacIntyre writes about living out a life based on Nietzsche's assumptions: "The price paid for liberation from what appeared to be the external authority of traditional morality," for example, is that "each moral agent" is now on his or her own, speaking "unconstrained by the externalities of divine law, natural teleology or hierarchical authority."[16] This is precisely the posture Nietzsche wanted to propose.

"Why should anyone else now listen," MacIntyre asks, to these self-appointed authorities? If there is no supreme agent of authority, there is no way to determine who is right. "For each of us is taught to see himself or herself as an autonomous moral agent; but each of us also becomes engaged by modes of practice, aesthetic or bureaucratic, which involve us in manipulative relationships with others."[17] When we deny all ultimate authority, this is the way we must behave in human community. We are inevitably pitted against one another. We battle for the "power of consecration," to use David Brooks's felicitous term, the power to determine what is right and wrong, true and good.

As Nietzsche understood so well, it all comes down to power. When there is no story that pulls us all together, to which we yield in trust; when there is no authority to which we can turn to decide which argu-

---

[16] Alasdair MacIntyre, *After Virtue: A Study in Moral Theory* (Notre Dame: University of Notre Dame Press, 1981), p. 68.
[17] Ibid.

ment negotiates reality better than another, then it is all about power—the power of argument, even the power of guns in the end. Indeed, the "army of metaphors" we once regarded as the truth collapse in a heap, once God vanishes from sight.

"Whither is God?" Nietzsche asked famously.

> I shall tell you. We *have killed him*—you and I. All of us are his murderers. But how have we done this? How were we able to drink up the sea? Who gave us the sponge to wipe away the entire horizon? What did we do when we unchained this earth from its sun? Whither is it moving now? Whither are we moving now? Away from all suns? Are we not plunging continually? Backward, sideward, forward, in all directions? Is there any up or down left? Are we not straying as through an infinite nothing?[18]

Once God is dead, we are free-floating, on our own, cut off from the anchoring center. We are in a world of colliding maps. Are we plunging downward, going backward, moving forward? There is no way to know, because there is no center, no compass, no authority, no tradition. We are "straying as through an infinite nothing."

"God is dead," says Nietzsche. "God remains dead. And we have killed him. How shall we, the murderers of all murderers, comfort ourselves? What was holiest and most powerful of all that the world has yet owned has bled to death under our knives." And to those who continue to worship this dead God in churches, Nietzsche has this word of scorn: "What are these churches now if they are not the tombs and sepulchers of God?"[19] Such is the voice of the "man of renunciation," the voice of one who would deny everything.

How could our culture have come to this? Fish wants to sanitize Nietzsche's language, but in the end, he says much the same thing: "By the end of the nineteenth century, human authority has been put in the place of revelation; or rather human authority, now identified with the progressive illumination afforded by reason, has become the vehicle of revelation and of a religion that can do very nicely without any strong

---

[18]Nietzsche, *The Portable Nietzsche*, p. 95.
[19]Ibid., p. 96.

conception of personal deity."[20]

I think it is fair to ask whether we are doing "very nicely" as a culture and a world without God. When God is relegated to our private musings alone, irrelevant to anything public, anything cultural, marginalized if not banished from public discourse about anything that matters—does that make things better? Do we really believe in this "progressive illumination afforded by reason" alone? Is this the god in whom we place our ultimate trust? And then the huge question for our purposes: Could Nietzsche's notion of a world without God possibly lie as the animating center of our universities? Is that the kind of university we really want? Surely this is not the bread we have to offer our students and to a world that comes asking for bread. Surely we must conclude that we are not doing very nicely.

Maybe there is another way. Surely there is an alternative.

[20]Fish, "Why We Can't All Just Get Along."

8

A WORLD WITHOUT EASTER

*History is driven, over the long haul, by culture—by what men
and women honor, cherish, and worship; by what societies deem
to be true and good, and by the expressions they give to those
convictions in language, literature, and the arts; by what individuals
and societies are willing to stake their lives on.*

GEORGE WEIGEL

ONE EASTER MORNING I PADDED OUT my front door very early to
pick up my newspapers, and I found myself, as a Christian on this most
holy of days, exuberant and expectant. It was a beautiful day in Seattle,
the sun slanting early on the trees and the flowers blooming wildly.
This is the day, I thought, when two billion Christians all over the
globe will shout and sing that our Lord is risen, all of us caught up in
the profound mystery that changed everything. This morning we cel-
ebrate the extraordinary center of a grand drama that continues to unfold on this very Easter morning in the twenty-first century.

Back inside, with a Starbucks latte in hand, I began to scan through
my papers—the *New York Times* and the *Seattle Times*—and suddenly I
realized there was *not one word* about Easter in these papers. The Seattle paper ran a rather strange article about off-beat notions of prayer,
something intended, I guess, as a kind of grudging, glancing notice
that something religious was going on this day. But it wasn't Easter the
writer was talking about. People don't go to church in our region, this
writer reminded us again, but they do pray, even if in strange and unconventional ways. When it comes to Easter, there was a glaring ab-

sence. Neither one of these papers wanted to talk about Easter.

With two billion Christians in the world, how can it be that there is no mention in our papers that Easter is news on Easter morning? Millions of Americans went to see *The Passion of the Christ*, and yet no mention of Easter in our papers. The leading cultural voices of our time would just as soon airbrush Easter right off our cultural and personal maps. It's okay to indulge such stuff in private or in little groups off to the margins, but please keep your personal enthusiasms to yourselves. Apparently, Easter does not mean anything to the editors of the *New York Times* or the *Seattle Times*, or, they suppose, to their readers. This is not the real stuff of public life.

Where are we going when the Christian story is banished from our common, public scene? What will happen to our culture when we cut ourselves off from our roots, an earth unhinged from our sun, as Nietzsche put it? These are roots that have nourished a decent society, with some exceedingly important values that have held together a healthy civilization. Can those values be sustained when they are finally and thoroughly disconnected from the roots of faith and the people of Easter that have nourished them throughout history?

We are watching the deconstruction of our history, the writing of a new story in decidedly secular terms; with relentless, sometimes thoughtless, breathtaking speed, we are headed toward a culture in the West we know very little about, a culture without roots in the Christian story. This is the extraordinary cultural shift we have been examining, what the philosopher Charles Taylor calls a "titanic change in our western civilization," where "the presumption of unbelief has become dominant." This is a view of the world, he adds, that "has achieved hegemony in certain crucial [subcultures], the academic and intellectual life" chief among them.[1]

———————————— ■ ————————————

When John G. Roberts was nominated in July 2005 to become the

[1]Charles Taylor, *A Secular Age* (Cambridge, Mass.: Belknap Press of Harvard University Press, 2007), pp. 12-13.

chief justice of the United States, there was a flurry of concern among some politicians and the major media that he would become too much a conservative influence on the court. Some of that concern, however, focused on his life as a devout Catholic. Why should this be a concern, one might ask? Roberts and his wife, both of them apparently sincere Christians, were constantly in the spotlight precisely because they were Christians. Roberts was asked, quite bluntly at times, if religion would get in the way of performing his duties faithfully on the Supreme Court. He was scrutinized intensely: Would he be willing and able to keep his faith, as Peter Steinfels of *The New York Times* said at the time, "separate from his legal judgments"? One priest, who knew the couple well, even suggested that their faith "would affect their personal lives, but they are very professional in their work." Does this mean that faith, if it were allowed to seep into public responsibilities, might cloud clear thinking or muddy the waters of the wise discernment required of a Supreme Court justice? Does it mean that the Christian faith really has no place on the Supreme Court?

Steinfels suggested the ideal for him and for the culture in which we live is "a warm but conventionally contained religious faith," a faith that must stay tightly contained in the private sphere and must be fiercely guarded on all fronts from contaminating one's pure, professional performance. "This dichotomy between the personal and the public comes naturally to a Western culture that for half a millennium has been gradually freeing areas like law, science, medicine, politics and economics from direct oversight by religion," Steinfels writes.[2]

This is true, but it is worth asking if law, science, medicine, politics and economics have been better off, freed from any influence of religion or people of faith. Isn't this something like Nietzsche unchaining the earth from its sun? And further, we are really not fretting here about "direct oversight" of religion. What in the world could that mean in our day and age? Never in our history in America have we had anything close to "direct oversight by religion" in any matter of public arrangement.

---

[2]Peter Steinfels, "The Roberts Nomination Raises the Issue of the Role of Religious Faith in Public and Professional Life," *The New York Times*, July 30, 2005, sec. A13.

No, what we are really fretting about, persistently and constantly, as a society is the fear that religion might have any influence at all in the things that really matter. We seem mortified that someone's faith might somehow come out into the open and actually make a difference in the performance of his or her public or professional duty.

How have we come to this? We are close here to living in a culture that is hell-bent on airbrushing the influence of Christian faith and conviction out of the public arena, even out of our history, certainly out of our universities. We are trying valiantly to drive Christians into exile. What nonsense that a Christian could or should eliminate one's deepest personal convictions from informing judgment or performance, and yet that is precisely what is suggested in this public discussion. How is it possible that we have come to this, that we must relegate all matters of faith to the private sphere to keep the public somehow untainted, as if that could ever be possible, or desirable? With Yale law professor Stephen Carter and so many others, I contend this is not what our American founders had in mind when they established the separation of church and state, and yet this is what we have come to culturally.[3]

Lesslie Newbigin places part of the blame for this bifurcation between the public and the private spheres on Christians throughout modern history: "The response of the Christian churches—or at least the Protestant churches—to the challenge of the Enlightenment was to accept the dichotomy and withdraw into the private sector. Having lost the battle to control education, and having been badly tattered in its encounter with modern science, Christianity in its Protestant form has largely accepted relegation to the private sector, where it can influence the choice of values by those who take this option."[4] That last line might be rephrased to say that Christians have accepted the marginal posture of influencing values *only* for those who are Christians. We simply accept that our role is to preach to the choir.

---

[3]See Stephen L. Carter, *The Culture of Disbelief: How American Law and Politics Trivialize Religious Devotion* (New York: Basic Books, 1993), for an outstanding clarification of the notion of separation of church and state. Our current notion, Carter contends, is not what was intended.

[4]Lesslie Newbigin, *Foolishness to the Greeks: The Gospel and Western Culture* (Grand Rapids: Eerdmans, 1986), p. 19.

We have come to feel that we have very little to say, especially when it comes to shaping culture. To imagine that this great, historic faith tradition should have nothing to say about justice in our legal system or wisdom in our educational enterprise or the ethics of our business world is quite extraordinary—indeed it is a deconstructing of Western history. It is a misunderstanding of our posture as Christians throughout history, a misunderstanding of the way Christians have sought to engage the culture, all the while valiantly seeking to make the world a better place.

What is the Christian to do? Are we to be satisfied with preaching to the choir only? Newbigin says, "The claim, the awesome and winsome claim of Jesus Christ to be alone the Lord of all the world, the light that alone shows the whole of reality as it really is, the life that alone endures forever—this claim is effectively silenced. It remains, for our culture, just one of the varieties of religious experience," a weak and distant voice shuffled off to the margins of public, social and cultural influence.[5] Somehow we have accepted our posture of exile.

Surely this can't be the end of the story. Surely we are not called by the Christian gospel to sit on the sidelines of our culture. Complacency about this marginalized position, acceptance of a posture of silence— this surely is not the way things are supposed to be. No, rather, it is our calling in this post-Nietzsche, postmodern, post-Christian world to keep the claims of Christ as Lord out in the open, never planted under the bushel basket that Jesus himself talked about.

———————————— ∎ ————————————

In the early part of the twentieth century, the great American writer Flannery O'Connor spent time thinking and writing about a culture without Easter. As she observed her world of the American South, she tells us over and over again, in brilliant, startling, often jolting stories, that the consequences of a world without Easter are not pretty.

[5]Ibid., p. 19.

In one of the greatest short stories in all American literature, "A Good Man Is Hard to Find," O'Connor brings us into contact with the Misfit, a man of renunciation, just like Nietzsche. As the story begins, this incorrigible and exceedingly dangerous convict is in the news, having escaped from prison and now on the loose. Suddenly, we encounter a collision, both literal and figurative, when a normal, middle-class Southern family, off for vacation in the family car, veers off the map and then off the road, their car flipping into a ditch. This turn of plot happens when the family cat leaps from its cage, claws unsheathed, and lands on the neck of Bailey, the father, who is driving. This is one of those startling disruptions of the normal for which O'Connor is famous.

Then, from the bluff overlooking the scene of the accident, the Misfit and his buddies appear. At this moment, this ordinary family, having escaped the tragedy of accidental death, now faces an existential encounter with a world without Easter. One map of the world collides with another. It is as if we witness, at the fulcrum of this story, the hinge moment of history we have been talking about.

The Misfit feels compelled to launch the chilling, cold-blooded killing of this innocent family, and as he does, he reflects in conversation with the grandmother on the resurrection of Jesus, of all things. "The resurrection changed everything," the Misfit muses, as he sits on the ground with the grandmother of the brood, his gun in his hand. The sound of shots pierce the air from offstage in the woods somewhere, as his buddies shoot her children and grandchildren one by one. What a horrifying moment for the grandmother, and yet the Misfit continues calmly to reflect that when Jesus was raised from the dead, "he thown everything off balance." After Easter, nothing could ever be the same, and so we'd better make up our minds about this pivotal moment in history. This choice is crucial, both personally and for our culture, says the Misfit.

And here is the Misfit's premise:

> "If He did what He said, then it's nothing for you to do but thow away everything and follow Him, and if He didn't, then it's nothing for you to do but enjoy the few minutes you got left the best way you can—by killing somebody or burning down his house or doing some other mean-

ness to him. No pleasure but meanness," he said and his voice had become almost a snarl.[6]

At this point the grandmother reaches out in a moment of motherly sympathy to touch this cold-blooded man of renunciation. While her heart had been encased in a huge amount of complacency, self-centeredness, even self-righteousness, quite selfishly protecting herself from any vulnerability, she responds to what she thinks might be an opening for tenderness and her own survival. But as she reaches out to touch the Misfit, suggesting that he is like one of her own babies, he recoils like a snake and shoots her through the chest.

The Misfit must deny everything, including a tender touch. He must deny affection and meaning and purpose and hope for the future. He knows it matters hugely when one denies the Jesus of the resurrection, the Easter moment of history, the Easter moment of personal choice, and he has made his own decisive choice to go it alone.

Denial is the way to go. It is impossible to trust anyone, including the great story of the ages, the Easter story, that dramatic moment in history when the doors of mystery and meaning opened wide into new dimensions of human flourishing. Jesus rose from the dead, and, as the Misfit knows, if that is true, everything changes. The Misfit understands at some profound level that how one responds to this extraordinary moment in time makes all the difference. He cannot trust what he cannot see, in the end, and of course the consequences are brutal. "No pleasure but meanness," he says, defining a map for himself. We are not doing very nicely, O'Connor would say to Fish and Nietzsche, when Easter is airbrushed out of our lives and off the map of our lives and our culture.

━━━━━━━━━━━━━━━ ∎ ━━━━━━━━━━━━━━━

The provocative Catholic intellectual George Weigel reflects in a number of places about the "secularization in Western Europe." He knows

---

[6]Flannery O'Connor, "A Good Man Is Hard to Find," *A Good Man Is Hard to Find and Other Stories* (New York: Harcourt Brace Jovanovich, 1955), p. 28.

that this process, reaching back into the nineteenth century, has had "profound public consequences." To airbrush Easter out of existence, to cut out the roots of European history, has produced "crucial, indeed lethal, consequences for European public life and European culture." Weigel quotes Christopher Dawson: "A secular society that has no end beyond its own satisfaction is a monstrosity—a cancerous growth which will ultimately destroy itself."[7]

Europe has drawn up a new constitution, and many political and intellectual leaders from many nations have argued fiercely that there should be no mention of Christian influence on Europe's past. Weigel asks, "Why have many of Europe's political leaders insisted that the new Constitution for Europe includes a deliberate act of historical amnesia, in which a millennium and a half of Christianity's contributions to the European understanding of human rights and democracy are airbrushed from the continent's political memory?"

Weigel says, "To deny that Christianity had anything to do with the evolution of free, law-governed, and prosperous European societies is more than a question of falsifying the past; it is also a matter of creating a future in which moral truth has no role in governance, in the determination of public policy, in understandings of justice, and in the definition of that freedom which democracy is intended to embody."[8] Indeed, when we cut off the Christian roots that shaped and sustained the culture we enjoy, we are writing a new story that will define a new way of life, a new and uncertain kind of future.

So many of the significant values we enjoy as a Western culture—values that have made us a decent society, even in spite of our great failures—values such as individual freedom, freedom to practice religion (any religion), liberty for all, respect for human dignity, respect for women, equality, kindness, civility, care for the poor, personal rights, the rule of law, the right to elect our leaders and the separation of church and state—it is not too much to say that most all of this emerged out of the faith tradition and the wisdom of people who believed that the Jesus of Easter changed everything.

[7]George Weigel, "Europe's Problem—and Ours," *First Things* 140 (February 2004): 23.
[8]Ibid.

When we look at this list of personal, social and cultural values, we must, of course, appropriately focus on the many painful ways we have fallen short of these aspirations. But the only way of judging our failures is by the set of standards *informed by these very values*. We cannot lose sight of the fact that without Christian influence, these values have no authority to give them substance and force. And so it seems baffling that we are now trying frantically and forcefully to eliminate the influence of Easter people from the culture in which we live. The warning here is that we just may lose the values that hold our lives together.

Weigel lifts up what he calls the "Slavic view of history," established by poets, novelists, intellectuals, and religious and political leaders from Poland and other parts of Eastern Europe, including Karol Wojtyla, who later became Pope John Paul II, and Vaclav Havel, poet and president of the Czech Republic. Here we find that "genuine 'revolution' means the recovery of lost spiritual and moral values." Weigel says,

> The common thread running through these disparate thinkers is the conviction that the deepest currents of history are spiritual and cultural, rather than political and economic. . . . History is driven, over the long haul, by culture—by what men and women honor, cherish, and worship; by what societies deem to be true and good, and by the expressions they give to those convictions in language, literature, and the arts; by what individuals and societies are willing to stake their lives on.[9]

Poland survived brutal Nazi invasion and oppressive Soviet occupation and the attempted reinvention of culture and society. Weigel says,

> Better Poland prevailed—because of culture: a culture formed by a distinctive language . . . ; by a unique literature, which helped keep alive the memory and idea of "Poland"; and by the intensity of its Catholic faith. Poles know in their bones that culture is what drives history over the long haul.[10]

In *The Clash of Civilizations and the Remaking of the World Order*,

---

[9]Ibid., p. 21.

[10]George Weigel, *The Cube and the Cathedral: Europe, America, and Politics Without God* (New York: Basic Books, 2005), p. 31.

Samuel P. Huntington says something similar about the importance of culture:

> In the post-Cold War world, the most important distinctions among peoples are not ideological, political, or economic. They are cultural. . . . People define themselves in terms of ancestry, religion, language, history, values, customs, and institutions. They identify with cultural groups: tribes, ethnic groups, religious communities, nations, and at the broadest level, civilizations.[11]

And so it's all about culture. If we miss this point, we simply cannot make sense of the world, its history, the sustaining forces that drive us into the future, even the collisions of civilizations, cultures and religions. If we miss this point in our public debates or our educational enterprise from childhood through college and beyond, we simply will not be relevant to what's going on in the world. Equally true, if we persist in cutting ourselves off from the cultural and historical roots that have made us what we are, there is no way to know what the consequences will be.

Cutting free from our roots may seem liberating for the moment, but as we do, we are defining a different future, a different world, a different understanding of what we hold to be good and beautiful. Difficult though it may be to nurture roots in our postmodern world, without those roots we are like cut flowers, as the historian David McCullough said when he visited the Seattle Pacific campus in 2006. Cutting from our roots leaves us with nothing to offer in our inevitable encounter with other cultures, other civilizations. We will have no way of engaging in "the contest among cultures," as David Brooks phrases it, "over the power of consecration—the power to define what is right and wrong."[12] We are left with nothing but the collision of maps with no idea of where we are headed.

■

One final word on a culture without Easter: Soon after the death of

[11]Samuel P. Huntington, *The Clash of Civilizations and the Remaking of the World Order* (New York: Simon & Schuster, 1996), p. 2.
[12]David Brooks, "The Jagged World," *New York Times*, September 3, 2006, sec. C10.

Pope John Paul II, Weigel reflected on how the Pope so often focused on "the realm of culture." He encouraged Christians everywhere to be about the work of building up "vibrant public moral cultures capable of disciplining and directing the tremendous energies—economic, political, aesthetic, and, yes, sexual—set loose in free societies." The Pope understood that "a vibrant public moral culture is essential for democracy and the market, for only such a culture can inculcate and affirm the virtues necessary to make freedom work. . . . Building the free society certainly involves getting the institutions right; beyond that, however, freedom's future depends on men and women of virtue, capable of knowing, and choosing, the genuinely good."[13]

We need universities at the front edge of building up "vibrant public moral cultures." We need universities fully committed to educating "men and women of virtue," people "capable of knowing, and choosing" the good. These are alternative universities in our day. And this is the way we can reimagine our Christian universities: animated from the very core of their identity by the great mystery of Easter, these universities seek to build up vibrant, life-giving cultures by equipping men and women of virtue to choose the genuine good.

This is culture work, not political or ideological work. As James Davison Hunter says so clearly, "There are no political solutions to the problems most people care about."[14] He worries about "the politicization of everything." As Christians have turned to political power to speak the gospel into our culture, there has been "a narrowing of the complexity and richness of public life and with it, a diminishing of possibility for thinking of alternative ways to address common problems and issues."[15]

What we need to find is an approach that transcends our current obsession with politics as the only way we can publicly discuss what matters. Important as politics may be at times, they are not everything or even the most important thing. We've got to get this culture thing

---

[13]George Weigel, "Mourning and Remembrance," *Wall Street Journal*, April 4, 2005, sec. A14.
[14]James Davison Hunter, *To Change the World: The Irony, Tragedy, and Possibility of Christianity in the Late Modern World* (New York: Oxford University Press, 2010), p. 171.
[15]Ibid., p. 106.

right. We've got to equip young people in culture-savvy ways, understanding that in the end our potential to make the world a better place will only come through building up life-giving cultures. Indeed, this is the only way our Christian universities can be the place where world change begins.

9

SOMETHING WE'VE NEVER SEEN BEFORE

*I just have this feelin we're looking at somethin
we really aint never even seen before.*

<small>SHERIFF LAMAR IN CORMAC MCCARTHY, *NO COUNTRY FOR OLD MEN*</small>

A KIND OF SECULAR ORTHODOXY HAS settled into our culture for well over a century now, and the results are coming in. We look out across the landscape of our world, and we have to agree with old Sheriff Lamar in Cormac McCarthy's horrifying novel *No Country for Old Men*: "I just have this feelin we're looking at somethin we really aint never even seen before."[1]

Nietzsche's nihilism, says James Davison Hunter, "may not be all-pervasive but it is endemic to the late modern world." And furthermore, "it is not surprising . . . that for all the good that remains in the world and that we continue to create, there is much in the late modern world that generates meaninglessness, ugliness, estrangement, heartlessness, and outright cruelty."[2]

We must ask, then, if Stanley Fish and so many other secularists are right, that we "can do very nicely without any strong conception of personal deity." As we size things up in the world, can we call this an accurate assumption? "Human authority" and "progressive illumination" are supposed to take us to a new world of human flourishing, but isn't it fair to challenge this supreme confidence in this secular orthodoxy that guides the way for our culture? Something surely has changed.

---

[1]Cormac McCarthy, *No Country for Old Men* (New York: Knopf, 2005), p. 3.
[2]James Davison Hunter, *To Change the World: The Irony, Tragedy, and Possibility of Christianity in the Late Modern World* (New York: Oxford University Press, 2010), p. 264.

I think it is fair to say the old sheriff is on to something.

Nietzsche allows himself to contemplate the consequences of God's final departure from our world. If the act of murdering God is such an advantage to history, what then does our world look like? What are the consequences of killing God? What are the consequences, not only for our personal lives, but on the world stage as well? Nietzsche replies:

> You will never pray again, never adore again, never again rest in endless trust; you deny yourself any stopping before ultimate wisdom, ultimate goodness, ultimate power, while unharnessing your thoughts. . . . There is no avenger for you, no eventual improver; there is no reason any more in what happens, no love in what will happen to you; no resting place is any longer open to your heart, where it has only to find and no longer to seek; you resist any ultimate peace, you want the eternal recurrence of war and peace. Man of renunciation, do you want to renounce all of this? Who will give you the necessary strength? Nobody yet has had this strength.[3]

This is the horrifying price when we have finally "unchained this earth from its sun," and yet for Nietzsche, this is the step we must take, the only courageous path. "God is dead," and this is the life we can anticipate. But it is not just the life we may imagine for each of us personally: We are left to contemplate what our world might look like built on such foundations. This is the stone our profoundly secular culture has to offer to those who come asking for bread. These are the consequences of this utter renunciation, though such consequences, for Nietzsche, are far better than living with "illusions." Although Nietzsche envisioned at this point that he was the one with strength enough to take such a path, he died a madman at the age of fifty-six.

■

We want to say our culture has not come to this. This sounds so awfully extreme. We want to say our culture may condemn God to death and

---

[3]Friedrich Nietzsche, *The Portable Nietzsche,* ed. and trans. Walter Kaufmann (New York: Penguin Books, 1954), p. 95.

elevate the courageous individual as lord of each separate map and yet still affirm values of decency, kindness, honesty and integrity. We want to believe we are doing very nicely and that we can build an even better world with the resources such a culture has to offer.

But even Nietzsche knew you can't have it both ways. You can't knock out the props of ultimate authority and still have a culture that promotes something true and good and beautiful *in common*. There is no way this will happen. If God is dead, he is dead. That is a fundamental presupposition of the culture. And when we impose this fundamental presupposition on our culture, in our organizations, in our political and social spheres, in our educational system, our universities; when we wipe out any authority or tradition in which we can commonly place our trust—well, the center cannot hold. The whole notion of common language and common values collapses. We have no choice but to withdraw into our own private spheres, from which we look out on a world of colliding maps.

We think about what happened in the streets of New York on that clear September morning in 2001. Our story of "human authority, now identified with the progressive illumination afforded by reason," as Fish puts it, was suddenly, dramatically tested. Something mysterious and horrifying ripped through our confidence. This felt like massive and bewildering regression rather than hopeful progression.

We may have believed that "progressive illumination afforded by reason" had helped to build those solid glass and steel structures in the center of one of the great cities of the Western world. Our old maps told us we could place our trust in inevitable progress, economic growth, safe cities, powerful global financial systems and transformative technology. Our old maps told us we could safely push to the margins any notion of religion as a guiding force in the world. If we thought about culture at all, we imagined only the trappings of entertainment, easy money, celebrity, luxurious lifestyles—all of it unhooked from any notion that religion had anything to do with it.

And then 9/11 happened. After that, we stood in the streets of the great cities of the Western world with secular maps that seemed no longer to make sense of the world. Something dramatically new had broken into our awareness. Those shining towers of progress and prosperity came crashing down into a heap of dust, a "heap of broken images," to use T. S. Eliot's phrase again. It all seemed to come as from another world beyond our comprehension, a failure of imagination, as the 9/11 Commission stated so vividly, altering forever the map we carry around with us.

And we discovered something else on that fateful and frightening day. As a secular culture we had built a pretty solid case that we could be, and should be, "neutral" on religion. Religion was at best only for the private spheres of our lives. And then we found out with startling clarity that there are people in the world who will actually lay down their lives for what they believe to be true. We had been hard at work airbrushing religion out of sight and out of mind, off the cultural maps that guide us. We found with disturbing clarity that religion matters to most people in the world and that if we have any chance of responding to these new forces and influencing the world anew, it will be at the level where religion informs and shapes culture.

To erase religion from the cultural maps of our world is not going to happen any time soon. We have a new reality we must deal with. But the question for our time is how to choose the most sure and true way. For this exceedingly challenging and sensitive task, I believe the university of our day is not equipped to provide much guidance, precisely because it professes that all questions of religion have been put to bed, brushed off into the private, personal sphere. And so here is where the Christian university must step up to what is perhaps the most important challenge of our day: affirming the more sure and true way in Jesus Christ while also engaging other faith traditions.

———————————————— ∎ ————————————————

The old sheriff in McCarthy's novel spends his days and nights trying to manage the human collisions on the borderlands of Texas and Mexico, down there where the great drug wars of our day are being fought. The sheriff has a map of the world that has guided him in his long public service in this scruffy, barren land. But the world has changed, dramatically changed.

This seasoned sheriff and his buddies, those who had been able to say "we've seen it all," find themselves suddenly in a world full of "misfits," the likes of which they have never seen before. This is a disturbing new breed of people willing and capable of inflicting a kind of violence that is profoundly and horrifyingly new. These borderland cops find themselves in a world of utter disregard for human dignity and human life. The map Sheriff Lamar carries around with him can't seem to locate where he is or where he needs to go. Bewilderment, resignation and horror set in. Indeed, this is no country for old men who were educated to read only the maps of an earlier time.

There is a new breed out there, the sheriff discovers, a new kind of human being armed with enormous sums of money and the most sophisticated and lethal technology ever to exist. These are people with no connections, no borders, no loyalties and no overarching story that makes sense of their lives and gives them hope for the future. The clash of wills is everything. The battle is all there is. This is a world where power of the rawest sort wins. This is Nietzsche's world. God is dead, to be sure.

Sheriff Bell, another seasoned sheriff trying to grasp the culture of these new borderlands, talks about a nineteen-year-old man who killed a fourteen-year-old girl. The papers said it was a crime of passion. Sheriff Bell says, "But he told me there wasnt no passion to it. [He] said he knew he was goin to hell. Told it to me out of his own mouth. I don't know what to make of that. I surely don't. I thought I'd never seen a person like that and it got me to wondering if maybe he was some new kind."[4] This kid's language, to the old sheriff, comes out of an inexplicable culture, and the sheriff needs a translator. He needs a new map to navigate his way toward something that makes sense.

The violence in McCarthy's haunting novel may seem far removed from the comfortable lives in which most of us live. But this is a signal of the kind of world we are creating when "any strong conception of personal deity" is taken off the maps of our understanding of human life and the human community.

---

[4]McCarthy, *No Country*, p. 3.

When we look into so many corners of our world, what we see is not very pretty. And we ask ourselves what we can do about it. We ask ourselves whether the university of our day is prepared to address these deeply troubling issues, or at least to address the cultural backdrop out of which these new realities spring. We ask ourselves if the construct of a pervasive secular orthodoxy can contain or guide what we see all around us. We witness with the old sheriffs the results of fallen human nature estranged from a loving and demanding God who wants so much more for his children. We yearn for a vision for our culture that is rooted in a God who defines a clear path out of our fallenness toward healing, wholeness and human flourishing.

What if the Christian university we are imagining were to look straight into this Nietzschean horror and propose another way?

10

THE CITY AND THAT EVER-ELUSIVE CERTAINTY

He doesn't doubt that in years to come, the coding mechanism will be known, though it might not be in his lifetime. . . . The brain's fundamental secret will be laid open one day.

FROM SATURDAY BY IAN MCEWAN

People are in a kind of suspended alarm, waiting for the future to unspool and not expecting it to unspool happily. . . . People sense something slipping away, a world receding, not only an economic one but a world of old structures, old ways and assumptions.

PEGGY NOONAN

THE OLD SHERIFFS IN *NO COUNTRY FOR OLD MEN* look out across the landscape of those desert border towns of Texas with bewilderment and resignation. Something has fundamentally changed. What do all the old habits of the heart with which they were educated and trained—things like courage and honesty and loyalty and order—matter in this new world? This is indeed not a country for these decent old men.

While the extreme, jolting violence of McCarthy's world may seem distant and not very relevant to our comfortable daily lives, these old men bring us face to face with a reality that does not square with the maps we have been carrying around. Bewilderment sets in. Seismic shifts of culture are taking place, and we are uncertain about what it means and what to do about it.

"People are in a kind of suspended alarm, waiting for the future to unspool and not expecting it to unspool happily," Peggy Noonan wrote in 2009. There is "a pervasive sense of anxiety, as though everyone feels they're on thin ice." Then she says something remarkable: "People sense something slipping away, a world receding, not only an economic one but a world of old structures, old ways and assumptions."[1]

How then do we educate when the ground seems to be shifting so dramatically and persistently? How do we locate a story of enduring, overall meaning? Even more importantly, what exactly is that story? If the university is to have any credibility in this world that seems to be unspooling unhappily, these are the questions it must address.

It might be helpful to open yet another novel of our time to examine further this sense of "something slipping away," this sense that the old structures, old ways and old assumptions are receding. This time we turn to the streets of London, in Ian McEwan's marvelous novel *Saturday*, where we find this same kind of bewilderment and resignation.

We enter the life of a successful neurosurgeon, Henry Perowne, as he makes his way through an ordinary yet extraordinary Saturday. Henry is the quintessential rationalist. He would enthusiastically endorse Stanley Fish's secularist view of "progressive illumination afforded by reason." Here is a man of our times: trained to peer into the intricacies of the human brain; trained to place everything under the microscope of human reason; trained in the orthodoxy of his culture and his profession to believe that if only given time, we will most certainly sort through the remaining mysteries of human life and even the seemingly intractable, troubling issues of our day. Answers are on the way, Henry believes. Bewilderment and resignation cannot be the

---

[1]Peggy Noonan, "There's No Pill for This Kind of Depression," *Wall Street Journal*, March 13, 2009, sec. A9.

final posture for someone like Henry.

But certainty grows more elusive as Henry confronts, and is confronted by, a world troublingly out of whack. How to make sense of violence and homelessness in the streets—violence that intrudes ultimately, shockingly, into the flat where Henry and his family live. How to make sense of a new global terrorism that seems poised to erupt into the streets of his beloved London. Henry's faith that rational answers are on the way is severely tested as we move through his Saturday.

Just imagine a hundred years ago, Henry muses. Imagine some middle-aged doctor like himself, taking stock of the scene before him in the streets of London. "You might envy this Edwardian gent all he didn't yet know," Henry thinks. "What was their body count, Hitler, Stalin, Mao? Fifty million, a hundred? If you described the hell that lay ahead, if you warned him, the good doctor—an affable product of prosperity and decades of peace—would not believe you."[2]

We hear in these musings a growing awareness on Henry's part of a world where something is slipping away, a world where chaos, violence and suffering threaten to intrude. But what to do when you hold out hope in progressive illumination that all will be well if we just let human authority have its way? The odds don't seem good to Henry as he walks the streets of contemporary London, yet his training and his deep secular presuppositions cause him to press against the odds. All will be right someday, he seems to be saying. Give us time to think things through.

At one moment in the novel, while Henry is deeply engrossed in the exceedingly delicate maneuvers of piercing the brain of a patient, he reflects that "for all the recent advances, it's still not known how this well-protected one kilogram or so of cells actually encodes information, how it holds experiences, memories, dreams and intentions." What are these deep-down things that make up human life and experience? Do they elude the confident probing of the surgeon's knife and the musing of the confident materialist? Is there something in human experience that is out of reach from the scientist's final explanation? As we take the secularist's probe to its farthest reach in the intricacies of the human

---

[2]Ian McEwan, *Saturday* (New York: Doubleday, 2005), p. 286.

brain as well as in the complexities on the streets of our cities, we discover a human reality that needs to be explained in another way. We need *something more* to make sense of it all.

But just wait for a time; we will get it figured out, Henry continues to believe. The marvels of science and the tools of the master surgeon may not have provided a complete explanation. At least not yet. But Henry "doesn't doubt that in years to come, the coding mechanism will be known, though it might not be in his lifetime. Just like the digital codes of replicating life held within DNA, the brain's fundamental secret will be laid open one day. But even when it has, the wonder will remain, that mere wet stuff can make this bright inward cinema of thought, of sight and sound and touch bound into a vivid illusion of an instantaneous present, with a self, another brightly wrought illusion, hovering like a ghost at its centre."[3]

This is the ambivalence we continue to manage in our culture today. On the one hand, the brain is a work of astonishing beauty. It is hard to comprehend that this mere "wet stuff" can actually create so many marvelous wonders of vibrant human life. But on the other, the quintessential scientist must in the end regard it all as an illusion: life is nothing more than this clump of cells and digital codes. In the end, the materialist will bring wonder and mystery down to size.

But Henry continues to bump into things that do not slip easily into line with this view of life. As he looks out and sees the wandering homeless, for example, and the hopelessly mentally afflicted, he becomes "the professional reductionist." He "can't help thinking it's down to invisible folds and kinks of character, written in code, at the level of molecules." People are doomed by a "knot of affliction."[4] That's the scientist's elegant explanation, to which we are attracted. But we get the feeling that Henry does not fully believe such an explanation holds enough power. There is mystery here he can't quite penetrate. There must be some other, more fully human, response to the suffering of the poor, the lame and the mentally troubled. There must be some bread to offer that exceeds the stone of the cold explanations of philosophical materialism.

---

[3]Ibid., p. 262.
[4]Ibid., pp. 281-82.

Finally, in a climactic moment of the novel, two thugs invade the family comfort of Henry's London flat. Suddenly and inexplicably, Henry and his whole family come face to face with the violence and disorder of the streets. The comfort and seeming safety of their own beautiful space is invaded, violated. At this existential moment of human collision, Henry's faith in human authority alone has no meaning. An explanation for why this is happening to his family is beyond his imagination, beyond the powers of the quintessential rationalist. His map is suddenly and permanently being redrawn as the whole family faces violent, personal destruction. Henry's daughter, Daisy, is ordered by one of the thugs, who holds a knife to the throat of her mother, to strip from her clothes in front of the family. The intruders demand that she read a poem, of all things, and she chooses to recite, from memory, Matthew Arnold's "Dover Beach."

Here we are asked by the novelist to reflect on the meaning of "Dover Beach," 150 years after its publication. With all that has transpired in history in between, now that the "sea of faith" has most completely withdrawn from the scene, we find ourselves on Arnold's "darkling plain." As Daisy, standing there nakedly vulnerable, recites Arnold's lines, "even in this state, Henry balks at the mention of a 'sea of faith' and a glittering paradise of wholeness lost in the distant past."

Henry balks because he has accepted his culture's presupposition that such faith has always been an illusion. At this moment, Arnold's poem "rings like a musical curse," an indictment perhaps on the scene that unfolds before his eyes. "The plea to be true to one another sounds hopeless in the absence of joy or love or light or peace or 'help for pain.' . . . The poem's melodiousness, he decides, is at odds with its pessimism."[5]

At the end of Henry's ordinary-yet-extraordinary day in London, a long way from Arnold's reflections and yet tied by a thread of cultural continuity, "All he feels now is fear. He's weak and ignorant, scared of the way consequences of an action leap away from your control and breed new events, new consequences, until you're led to a place you

---

[5]Ibid., p. 230.

never dreamed of and would never choose."[6]

Like Henry, we live in a changed world, bewildered as things seem to spiral out of our control and beyond our understanding. This, then, is all we are left with when the sea of faith has withdrawn, when we have denied all overarching stories that might give purpose, meaning and direction.

As Henry climbs into bed at the end of this Saturday—with all his success and comfort and the joy of family brought under a terrifying cloud of bewilderment by the circumstances of a world seemingly spun out of control—he nestles up to his wife, "her silk pajamas, her scent, her warmth, her beloved form," and drawing closer to her, he concludes, "There's always this." And then he thinks, before he finally sleeps, "And then: there's only this."[7]

———————————————— ∎ ————————————————

As Christian universities we must propose an alternative to such bewilderment. We know "there's always this," to be sure, and that is good, but we know there is also *something more.* Bewilderment cannot be the final answer. The cold conclusion of the philosophical materialist cannot be the final answer. Even the warmth of our personal comfort cannot be the final answer. To offer only these is to offer a stone to our world instead of bread.

Fully cognizant that bewilderment and resignation, confusion and fear, reign in the streets of our cities and in the deserts of our borderlands, as Christians we can still confidently sing out a story of mystery and radiance that reaches even beyond our imagination of what might be possible. We have a story to offer the world. Our story helps us grasp the extent of human failure and fallenness. Our story defines the path through Jesus Christ toward redemptive life, toward radiance and joy. Our task is to learn better all the time how to speak that story into such a world.

And this is precisely the task for today's Christian university: We

---

[6]Ibid., p. 287.
[7]Ibid., p. 289.

must propose and model an alternative way of living and learning, standing out on the leading edge of the culture, showing the way toward something profoundly *more*.

11

SHATTERING FIXED CONCLUSIONS

THE POWER OF THE IMAGINATION

Gentle verses written in the midst of horror declare themselves for life.

CZESLAW MILOSZ

*[We look for the] long-range signposts to a reality which
lies deeper in God's dark purposes than we normally imagine.*

N. T. WRIGHT

*These poets not only discerned the new actions of God that
others did not discern, but they wrought the new actions of God
by the power of their imagination, their tongues, their words.
New poetic imagination evoked new realities in the community.*

WALTER BRUEGGEMANN

IT'S TIME TO BEGIN TO DIG OUR WAY OUT of this cultural hole into
which we have fallen. It's time to begin to define the alternative view
of the world out of which we might craft an alternative university. I
want now to propose an alternative story that is full of hope, full of
joy, full of promise that might shape a better world. This is an alternative story that has something more to offer to our culture than suspicion, resignation and bewilderment. We can actually *embrace* such a
story with some measure of certainty that it is true. We want to sing

from the rooftops a story of what is true and good and beautiful—and ultimately to roll up our sleeves and go to work to make the world a better place for all of God's children.

For me, of course, this is the Christian story. And let us imagine now an alternative university that is animated from its very core by this story of human flourishing. I believe such a university can actually engage our culture of radical suspicion in ways that are excellent, sophisticated and winsome—to give our students a place to land, a place of affirmation and genuine hope. This university offers to students and to the world a powerful alternative story of human flourishing. And when the world comes asking for bread, it is my deep conviction that what we have to offer through these Christian universities is the satisfying bread of life.

The premise of this pivoting chapter rests on the *power of the imagination*. I am not talking here about some vague notion of the imagination, but about what Walter Brueggemann calls the "biblical imagination." This imagination is framed, informed and infused by the expectations and anticipations of Scripture. This is the imagination that is radically open to the promptings of God's Spirit, the imagination that sees in ways beyond seeing, the imagination that discovers illuminating signals of the Spirit breaking out of the ordinary.

When N. T. Wright says that "[as we look for the] long-range signposts to a reality which lies deeper in God's dark purposes than we normally imagine," we are delighted and challenged to get on with the task.[1] But how might we begin? And why and where is this sacred reality hiding in our day? Do God's deep and dark purposes actually reside somewhere hidden from our view? We want to know that reality, despite secular dogmatists' statements to the contrary. We want to know if that reality promises *something more* for our lives and for the world.

But how do we spot the "signposts"? Can we be trained for this kind of attentiveness? Our tools for watchfulness have surely gone rusty, and yet we are not willing to buy the assumption that no signposts exist. And what is the language we can use to talk about such extraordinary discovery?

---

[1]N. T. Wright, *Paul: In Fresh Perspective* (Minneapolis: Fortress, 2005), p. 150.

We need to imagine the *something more* that seems to lie obscured by the secularist landscape of absence. We must use the power of our imagination to discover signs of the sacred in the ordinary—the first step as we go about the challenge of learning to announce the good news of the gospel. If we can nurture this kind of attentiveness, perhaps we can find our way to the whole redemptive story of God's love for his world and for all of his children.

Such an imagination was more active in times past, before we desacralized our world, before pervasive philosophical materialism took over. We need to cultivate, nourish and reclaim the power of the imagination to see beneath the surface of things, to see God's illuminating presence shining out when we least expect it. James Davison Hunter suggests that "cultural change is most enduring when it penetrates the structure of our imagination."[2] We must devote our energies to imagination formation as much as we care about intellectual formation or spiritual formation. This is a first-order requirement as we seek to change the world.

We need, as the New Testament scholar Richard Hays has said so beautifully, a "conversion of the imagination."[3] As seen in the life of the apostle Paul, such a conversion follows the transformation that happens when we are confronted with the living Jesus on our road to Damascus. That's what is needed for Christians in our culture—a radical conversion of the imagination so we might once again peer into the sacred dimensions of reality, affirming, confirming and announcing our story of good news. In a culture of denial and absence, we need, not so much the tools of apologetics, but to open ourselves to the power of a transformed imagination.

Let's zero in on this kind of imagination at work by looking closely at the work of several poets. First, I think of Gerard Manley Hopkins,

[2]James Davison Hunter, *To Change the World: The Irony, Tragedy, and Possibility of Christianity in the Late Modern World* (New York: Oxford University Press, 2010), p. 42.
[3]Richard Hays, *The Conversion of the Imagination: Paul as Interpreter of Israel's Scripture* (Grand Rapids: Eerdmans, 2005).

that provocative Jesuit priest of the late nineteenth century, who discovers dimensions of the sacred all around him. These discoveries bring delight, sometimes startling illumination and always compelling evidence that God is present in the world. Hopkins made these penetrating discoveries at the same time that Nietzsche was sweeping aside all notions of the sacred as sheer illusion. Hopkins saw something radically different. He saw an amazing reality breaking loose, cropping out, bursting forth. His poems are joyous, expectant, celebratory. They announce the surprising vibrancy and vitality of a world that God not only called into being but also called very good. Hopkins simply doesn't buy into Nietzsche's assumption that God is dead: he spots the signposts of something deeper, something more.

We might imagine Hopkins listening as Nietzsche proposed his radical, earthshaking questions: "Whither are we moving now?" asked Nietzsche. "Are we not plunging continually? Backward, sideward, forward, in all directions? Is there any up or down left? Are we not straying as through an infinite nothing?" As we have seen, after summarily declaring that "God is dead," Nietzsche concluded with this horrifying question: Isn't it true there is "no resting place . . . any longer open to your heart"?[4]

Hopkins might have replied to Nietzsche with something like this: "No, no, you don't get it, Nietzsche. You are looking only at the surface of things. There is something more, something at a deeper level, something ready to spring loose, something shining out all around us. All this is evidence that God is present, even now, even here. I hear your voice, but I don't accept it. It is through a transformed imagination that you might catch a glimpse of something more."

We see such an imagination at work in a poem like "God's Grandeur":

Generations have trod, have trod, have trod;
And all is seared with trade; bleared, smeared with toil;
And wears man's smudge and shares man's smell: the soil
Is bare now, nor can foot feel, being shod.[5]

---

[4]Friedrich Nietzsche, *The Portable Nietzsche*, ed. and trans. Walter Kaufmann (New York: Penguin Books, 1954), p. 95.
[5]Gerard Manley Hopkins, "God's Grandeur," in *The Norton Anthology of English Literature*, 6th

Hopkins was a realist about things. He recognized the drift of culture to discount, dismiss and bury the sacred. And yet for all this banishment of the sacred, Hopkins offers up a fundamental affirmation: "The world is charged with the grandeur of God. / It will flame out, like the shining from shook foil."[6] This is the starting point for Hopkins; this is an alternative presupposition to the one Nietzsche has offered. The poet is able to affirm something more precisely because he discovers even in the ordinary the illuminating presence of God: Hopkins says, "There lives the dearest freshness deep down things."[7] This requires no more a leap of faith than for Nietzsche to proclaim that we are "straying as through an infinite nothing." But if Hopkins is right, we are going to have a very different world and very different lives. In the end, we are going to educate in very different ways.

Hopkins concludes this marvelous poem with a beautifully gentle affirmation of the presence of God in our midst:

> And though the last lights off the black West went
> Oh, morning, at the brown brink eastward, springs—
> Because the Holy Ghost over the bent
> World broods with warm breast and with ah! bright wings.[8]

Though darkness may dominate our vision, the Spirit of God hovers over the world. That Spirit threatens to break into our attention, perhaps when we least expect it. "How do I know this is true?" the poet might ask. For one thing, we begin with a different set of presuppositions: "The world *is* charged with the grandeur of God," and therefore there *does* live "the dearest freshness deep down things." These are radical statements for a predominantly secular, desacralized world. These statements declare a different starting point.

But from this "deep down" beginning point, the imagination takes over. And, if we are guided by the imagination of someone like Hopkins, we witness *presence*, not absence. We see the "bright wings." We

---

ed., ed. M. H. Abrams et al. (New York: Norton, 1996), pp. 2127-28.
[6]Ibid., p. 2128.
[7]Ibid.
[8]Ibid.

see grandeur flaming out. And it is *God's* grandeur. Do you see it? It's real. It's true. And it makes all the difference.

———————————————— ∎ ————————————————

T. S. Eliot writes in *The Four Quartets* that "when there is distress of nations and perplexity" (perhaps one more way of describing our own time), just then we are called "to apprehend / The point of intersection of the timeless / With time."[9] And how do we go about this act of apprehension and attentiveness? Through the kind of imagination we are talking about, this transformed imagination.

As is well known, Eliot wrote his great masterpieces of modernism, in particular "The Love Song of J. Alfred Prufrock" and "The Waste Land," laying out for all to see what an utterly godless world might look like. It is as if he took Nietzsche's map of understanding reality and gave it powerful expression through the language of the gifted poet.[10] These poems were revolutionary, not only tremendous breakthroughs in literary style, but also expressions of the deep, brooding melancholy of this new age of the twentieth century where Nietzsche cast his huge shadow.

But later in life, Eliot embraced the Christian story he had so thoroughly rejected, converting to the Anglican faith of England, his adopted homeland. To the amazement and disappointment of intellectuals around him, he began to discover hints of the sacred—even in the context of the wasteland culture he had helped to create. He began to understand his new role as a poet, that he must probe and penetrate that "point of intersection of the timeless / With time."

If we could get at this intersection, we just might be able to address our moment of "distress of nations and perplexity." Was this not the way to tap into life-giving, refreshing new roots right in the middle of the wasteland of dryness and death that had so captured and frightened

[9]T. S. Eliot, "The Dry Salvages," *The Four Quartets* (New York: Harcourt, Brace & World, 1943), p. 44.
[10]T. S. Eliot, *The Waste Land and Other Poems* (New York: Harcourt, Brace & World, 1930), p. 30.

the culture? The power of the transformed imagination was a way forward.

To live at the point of intersection is hard work, Eliot says. It is "an occupation for the saint" that comes through "a lifetime's death in love, / Ardour and selflessness and self-surrender." This is the path of discipleship for the Christian, the path of Christian formation, the path of the spiritual disciplines, the experience of holiness and the life of community in worship. But don't carry any illusions here, because this is the way of the saint, the way of the contemplative, the work of the monk—and in this poem, Eliot opines that he is not sure he is up to such a task.

Nevertheless, we do get glimpses, and it is out of those glimpses that we simply *know* there is something more. Once we have opened ourselves up to those glimpses, we may enter into the life of discipline as Christians. What a conversion this must have been for Eliot, what a transformation! But listen to this evocative speech, and remember that such discovery and such language comes from a poet who, before his own conversion of the imagination, so convincingly described for us the landscape of sand and dryness and utter absence.

> . . . there is only the unattended
> Moment, the moment in and out of time,
> The distraction fit, lost in a shaft of sunlight,
> The wild thyme unseen, or the winter lightning
> Or the waterfall, or music heard so deeply
> That it is not heard at all, but you are the music
> While the music lasts. There are only hints and guesses,
> Hints followed by guesses; and the rest
> Is prayer, observance, discipline, thought and action.
> The hint half guessed, the gift half understood, is
> Incarnation.[11]

This marvelous text was written in 1941, after the great destruction of World War I that was so devastating for most intellectuals in Europe and America. This also was the time when the horrifying drama of World

---

[11]T. S. Eliot, "The Dry Salvages," *The Four Quartets* (New York: Harcourt, Brace & World, 1943), p. 44.

War II was unfolding across the European landscape. Nietzsche's nihilistic views of both life and culture had begun to settle in. And yet, at the same time, here is the great poet of modernism, probing that extraordinary moment when we get at least the "hints and guesses" of the illuminating radiance of God shining out from the ordinary world.

Once we have caught the hints, once we have guessed at the source, the only thing left is "prayer, observance, discipline, thought and action." This is a vision of affirmation in the very face of radical denial. This is the imagination powerfully at work discovering something more, something denied in our culture, and yet something real and vibrant and life-giving.

It is out of the discovery of this intersection, a discovery made possible by the imagination, that we have no choice but to imagine, articulate and then carry forward a radiant vision of flourishing for the world. Eliot believed we are following the hints and making the guesses, and that we are led, even if we only half understand, toward a realization of the incarnation of Christ, toward a world of presence, a world where the sacred surprisingly shines through the ordinary. This is what we have to offer to a skeptical, fully secular world: signs of God's presence in our midst.

•

We might also turn to the Polish-American poet Czeslaw Milosz to understand the work of the imagination in a dark time. Milosz lived through the bloody Nazi assault on his own country. He was then forced to endure the oppressive occupation of the Soviets as they went about creating their culture of lies in his country. How to engage such a culture? How to imagine something more in the face of these forces? What good was the imagination for such a time as this? Through it all, Milosz wrote poems. He talks about the enormous cost of exchanging "simplicity of the heart" for the sophisticated, restless mocking so prevalent in the elite, intellectual culture of modern Europe. One was forced to adopt a posture of suspicion, forced to grow cynical about all positions of affirmation, cynical about the sacred and certainly about religion. One could not afford to be simple. What good then was this act of writing poems? What possible good was this exercise of the imagination? Milosz believes that "gentle verses written in the midst of horror declare themselves for life."[12]

This strong and persistent poet wrote that "the sacred exists and is stronger than all our rebellions." Here is a deep presupposition: "the sacred exists," despite so many cultural and historical rumors to the contrary. The sacred asserts itself and is stronger than all our denials. Milosz was told by other intellectuals that it was "an abomination to write lyric poetry after Auschwitz." It was an intellectual, moral and spiritual escape, a copout. So, what drove him to continue to write "idyllic verses . . . in the very center of what was taking place . . . and not by any means out of ignorance"?[13]

Milosz stakes out a principle here, a posture: There is no justification for escape or separation from what is going on in the world. We are not allowed the luxury of separatism—as intellectuals or as Christians. We must look right into the face of it all, even into the horror, certainly into the grand sweep of uncertainty and suspicion. We are called by our faith in something more; we are called by our understanding of human nature, our mere living through the horror of history. If there is to be any hope in times of great darkness, chaos and fear, any hope of changing the world, the transformed imagination must stay active, Milosz believed, because it is the imagination that will discover the signposts of another way, the "hints and guesses" at something more. We are called to a mandate of sheer honesty.

"Evil grows and bears fruit," Milosz wrote, "which is understandable, because it has logic and probability on its side and also, of course, strength." But here is a message from the poet for such a time as this: "The resistance of tiny kernels of good, to which no one grants the power of causing far-reaching consequences, is entirely mysterious. . . . Such seeming nothingness not only lasts but contains within itself enormous energy."[14]

[12]Jeremy Driscoll, "The Witness of Czeslaw Milosz," *First Thing* 147 (November 2004): 33.
[13]Ibid.
[14]Ibid.

Through his restless and at times unconventional yet persistent Christian faith, Milosz's imagination was somehow shaped and formed by the good news of the gospel. Even if the forces of evil seem to overwhelm the signs of life, plant those "tiny kernels of good," because they are "entirely mysterious." We have no idea the power that resides in these evocative statements of the imagination.

Neither do we have any idea of the power of the gospel of Jesus Christ, winsomely and imaginatively articulated, to change the world. The forces of evil can at times overwhelm us. The power of a culture of denial and suspicion can sometimes dominate us. But we are reminded that the power of the good news is "entirely mysterious." Milosz concludes by saying that "one can draw momentous conclusions from this." To say the least. We too can conclude that power of the imagination is remarkable as we seek to bring the good news of the gospel into our world—to change the world.[15]

——————————————————— ■ ———————————————————

How do we learn to speak this way? How do we learn to evoke the powerful imagination in the face of forces that seem to overwhelm our best efforts to affirm something more, our best efforts to affirm anything at all? I want to propose that we align our thinking with the powerful tradition of the biblical imagination. This tradition can concretely help us as we seek to propose an alternative way of looking at the world. It can help us as we seek to redefine the Christian university for our day. It can provide the language we need to speak into a culture of deep suspicion and denial.

Old Testament scholar Walter Brueggemann says that the great poets of the Bible "not only discerned the new actions of God that others did not discern, but they wrought the new actions of God by the power of their imagination, their tongues, their words. New poetic imagination evoked new realities in the community."[16] How utterly ex-

---

[15]Ibid.

[16]Walter Brueggemann, *Hopeful Imagination: Prophetic Voices in Exile* (Philadelphia: Fortress, 1986), p. 2.

citing! Penetrating, probing, active discernment of a reality not seen by others—God's reality—this is the beginning point. But in the very act of speaking out of this imagination, these poets helped to shape the communities into which they were speaking.

In his book *Finally Comes the Poet: Daring Speech for Proclamation*, Brueggemann zeroes in on what he calls "the power of poetry." He illustrates that voices that speak out of this biblical imagination always speak into a reluctant and resistant culture. But they speak with such "shattering, evocative speech" that people must listen. This kind of speech "breaks fixed conclusions and presses us always toward new, dangerous, imaginative possibilities," Brueggemann says.[17] This is the breakthrough we are looking for.

Such an imagination will find another way of speaking. Such an imagination will speak the good news in such a way, for such a time as this, in such compelling and convincing ways, that its voice becomes "real and winsome," as Brueggemann says. Because it is real and winsome, it is "authorized and authorizing—in the face of ideologies that want to deny, dismiss, and preclude."[18] This is absolutely critical for our purposes. This is the kind of speech we must speak from the Christian university of our day—so that we might articulate into a desperate world a vision of human flourishing.

——————————————————— ∎ ———————————————————

Let's look at the biblical imagination at work. In a wonderful passage from Jeremiah, we see the power of the imagination actually becoming this "real and winsome" speech that can evoke "new realities in the community."

> They shall come and sing aloud on the height of Zion,
>   and they shall be radiant over the goodness of the Lord,
> over the grain, the wine, and the oil,
>   and over the young of the flock and the herd;

---

[17]Walter Brueggemann, *Finally Comes the Poet: Daring Speech for Proclamation* (Minneapolis: Fortress, 1989), p. 6.
[18]Ibid., p. 14.

their life shall become like a watered garden,
  and they shall never languish again.
Then shall the women rejoice in the dance,
  and the young men and the old shall be merry.
I will turn their mourning into joy,
  I will comfort them, and give them gladness for sorrow.
    (Jeremiah 31:12-13 NRSV)

Notice that the beginning point for Jeremiah's vision is the "goodness of the Lord." This bedrock presupposition is something like Hopkins's announcement that "the world is charged with the grandeur of God." Jeremiah's vision is for a better world, and such vision is grounded on the presupposition that God is good, that God will share his goodness freely, that God promises after sorrow there will be comfort, that life can be radiant. In the end, God will make all things right, all things new, and newness will look something like this.

From that starting point, that presupposition, comes an evocative imagining of what this radiant life might look like. There is gladness and joy, plenty and safety—all of which triumph over mourning and sorrow. We receive here an announcement of the promise that we "shall never languish again." Imagine that! Our contemporary world, a culture guided by suspicion and cynicism, will be quick to label such a vision idealistic at best, a Pollyannaish view of life. We will be told this is an illusion, that when placed up against the real world, this view promises only disappointment and discouragement and, in the end, despair.

But the poet will not be deterred by culture and history, by suspicion and denial. Courageously, Jeremiah looks right into the face of such denial and still affirms. This is the mark of the transformed imagination. The poet knows mourning, sorrow and languishing. The world of real imagination does not look away from unspeakable suffering and difficulty. It never ignores the consequences of our fallen nature. The biblical record demonstrates our ability to look into the face of horror and then, with courage and with the evocative power of language, to proclaim a radiant vision that the world can and will be made new, precisely because of the "goodness of the Lord."

Notice as well that biblical texts like this one from Jeremiah do not only "concern our relationship with God, decisive as that is," says Brueggemann. This is not just a promise of comfort, rescue and prosperity for an individual life, though it is that as well. In presupposing the "goodness of the Lord," we declare our personal relationship with God to be strong, real and vibrant. And we are reminded in worship, prayer and study of the goodness of the Lord to each of us.

But, as Brueggemann says, the vision of the biblical imagination is also an

> anticipation of the restoration of public life, safe cities, caring communities, and secure streets. . . . There is anticipation of the restoration of personal and interpersonal life, happy families, domestic well-being and joy, shared food and delighted relationships. Both public and interpersonal life depend on the self-giving action of God who makes newness possible.[19]

In the promise of the goodness of the Lord, we understand that God wants all of this for his children. This is a vision of human flourishing.

But what does the imagination have to do with this? Brueggemann goes so far as to say that "when the text comes to speak about this alternative life wrought by God, the text must use poetry. There is no other way to speak."[20] We are not talking about the language of conventional poetry, delightful though that might be. No, this poetry is the evocative language that comes from a transformed imagination. This is the imagination we must discover, cultivate and use. We talk often about Christian formation, spiritual formation and character formation; we would do well to learn the task of imagination formation.

The poet we are talking about casts a vision that is true, this vision of human flourishing. Brueggemann writes, "But we do not know concretely enough to issue memos and blueprints. We know only enough to sing songs and speak poems. That, however, is enough. We stake our lives on such poems."[21]

I submit that we might also build great universities on such poems.

---

[19]Ibid., p. 41.
[20]Ibid., p. 19.
[21]Ibid., p. 41.

We can build the strategies and write the memos, as we must, but first we must cast the vision through the language of the imagination. This is our starting point as we seek to imagine the Christian university of our day, a university where world change begins.

12

THE GOSPEL AND CULTURAL ENGAGEMENT

From whence comes the voice
that can challenge this culture on its own terms?

LESSLIE NEWBIGIN

I believe that part of the task of the church in our day
is to pioneer a way through postmodernity and out the other side,
not back to modernity in its various, even in its Christian, guises,
but into a new world, a new culture,
which nobody else is shaping and which we have a chance to.

N. T. WRIGHT

We need a new language for how the church engages the culture.

JAMES DAVISON HUNTER

THE LATE LESSLIE NEWBIGIN—PHILOSOPHER, theologian, missionary, both evangelical and ecumenical wrapped into one gracious, wise voice—is a model for me of how to lead and live as a Christian at the sometimes white-hot interface between culture and the gospel. Even though he was writing in the last part of the twentieth century, Newbigin may be one of the most important and helpful voices for our day on what it means to engage the culture with the gospel of Jesus Christ.

He can be our guide on questions of cultural engagement in our post-Enlightenment, postmodern, post-Christian and profoundly secular world.

Newbigin's *Foolishness to the Greeks: The Gospel and Western Culture* sits at the top of my list of required reading for all Christians and perhaps especially for those of us trying to define the Christian university for our time. Throughout the book, he persists with this central question: "From whence comes the voice that can challenge this culture on its own terms, a voice that speaks its own language and yet confronts it with the authentic figure of the crucified and living Christ so that it is stopped in its tracks and turned back from the way of death?"[1]

When I first read this question, I thought, *Yes, this is the challenge for our time, simply put.* And then I thought, *Yes, this is the question with which I must be involved in my life, in my leadership, in my abiding commitment to the Christian university.* "From whence comes the voice?" Can I be such a voice? Can the university in which I am deeply involved be such a voice?

Where does such a voice come from in our culture today? Do we hear this voice from our churches? Are they equipped to know the culture in such a way that they can speak its language effectively? Do our churches articulate the "authentic figure of the crucified and living Christ" into a culture that desperately yearns to hear this good news and yet, at the same time, seeks to airbrush the Christ of Easter off our cultural maps? And what about our Christian universities? Are we equipping our students with such a voice? Are we equipping them to be culture savvy? Are we providing for them an understanding of the gospel at the interface with the culture that defines so much of their lives? Let's think about this further.

Such a voice, Newbigin goes on to say, must be a voice "not of doom but of deliverance."[2] In other words, we must learn to speak not always out of confrontation but rather with a voice of hope and joy. It must be a voice that actually *speaks* into the culture, all the while crafting a vi-

---

[1]Lesslie Newbigin, *Foolishness to the Greeks: The Gospel and Western Culture* (Grand Rapids: Eerdmans, 1986), p. 9.
[2]Ibid., p. 10.

sion for a better world for all of God's children.

We often hear an admonition, attributed to St. Francis (though apparently mistakenly), that goes something like this: "Speak the gospel at all times—and when necessary use words." I have used that line many times when talking about the need to live out our faith in tangible, practical, visible ways. Our faith must be not just about words. We must learn always to walk the talk.

But we sometimes use this quote to let ourselves off the hook from actually speaking the good news with words. In the end, Christians are people of the Book. Our faith was spoken into being by the Word of God. For three thousand years and more, we have sought to articulate our understanding of God in words. We have debated, fiercely at times, the meaning of those words. We have interpreted those words differently during different historical moments. Clearly we must continue to learn how to speak the gospel into the culture, to be a voice. And so Newbigin is right to talk about learning a language of culture and the language of our faith so that we might become a voice that speaks clearly and effectively at the interface.

But we should take a step back and ask this question first: What is culture? James Davison Hunter gives us a good working definition, one Newbigin likely would applaud: "At the heart of culture is a complex of norms . . . better understood as commanding truths, which define the 'shoulds' and 'should nots' of our experience and, accordingly, the good and the evil, the right and the wrong, the appropriate and the inappropriate, the honorable and the shameful." This is culture: culture defines who we are as a certain group of people. "Put differently," says Hunter, "culture is a system of truth claims and moral obligations."[3] We are culture bound and culturally shaped.

But we should also be careful here. Does culture define everything? Is culture the final determinant of what we regard as true and good and

---

[3]James Davison Hunter, *To Change the World: The Irony, Tragedy, and Possibility of Christianity in the Late Modern World* (New York: Oxford University Press, 2010), p. 32.

beautiful? The question for Newbigin is how to *engage* this set of "complex norms," this "system of truth claims and moral obligations," with the gospel of Jesus Christ. This is an even more compelling task if we believe the norms, truth claims and moral obligations of culture need to be confronted. When we, as Christians, come to the conviction that the culture is on the wrong track, how do we turn that very culture "back from the way of death"? If we believe that the "authentic figure of the crucified and living Christ" is the story "not of doom but of deliverance," we must learn how to go about this complex work of engaging our culture.

——————————————— ■ ———————————————

Let's be clear about one other side of the question of culture. In our day, we are acutely aware of the influence and power of multiple cultures, both within our society and across the globe. So we must be very clear that we are talking about cultures, not just culture—cultures that are often in dramatic, even violent, conflict.

Our self-focused Western exclusiveness in education, in Christian teaching and in our understanding of the Scriptures has often narrowed our vision of the world dangerously. We are reminded these days by so many convincing voices—Lamin Sanneh, Joel Carpenter, Philip Jenkins and others—that God is doing new things in other parts of the world, things that seem out of focus when we attempt to view them through our Western-culture-bound understanding of the gospel and Scripture.

Newbigin spent some forty years on and off in India as a missionary. Perhaps this is why he is such a model of cultural engagement in a world of clashing and colliding cultures. This is what he believes: Such missionary experience, at its best, requires the *act of translation*. To engage, we have to learn to speak with sensitivity and nuance from one culture to another; indeed, we must learn the language of the other culture. And we have to be aware that "our gospel" is often culture bound too, with its own particular language. Because Christians have always been in the business of *culture*, or cultures, we have been in the business of *translation*. We must learn well the tools of translation if we are to be effective carriers of the good news.

When we talk about "culture," Newbigin says, we often refer to "the culture shared by the peoples of Europe and North America, their colonial and cultural off-shoots, and the growing company of educated leaders in the cities of the world." Today, of course, this is a controversial statement. We are reminded daily that we neglect other cultures of the world at great cost to a full understanding of the world. Even as we embrace the good news that God is doing a new thing in the global South—in Africa, Latin American and Asia, where the Christian church is exploding—we must admit that Newbigin is right: the culture of the modern, postmodern, secular West is the dominant, driving culture of the major cities of our world. This then remains the culture we must engage if we are to imagine effective translation of the gospel.

Yet our Western culture is under enormous stress and disturbance, tested and resisted, even viciously attacked from forces within and from all over the world. It may be in its early stages of demise. It is a culture sometimes separated from and ignorant of other cultures, sometimes arrogant, often humiliated in our day. But it still must be the beginning point in understanding the encounter between the gospel of Jesus Christ and the world in which we live. If we cannot translate the gospel into the profoundly secular culture in which we live in America and Europe, we have no chance to translate the gospel into other cultures of the world.

And so back to Newbigin's succinct statement. Where do we find this voice that can speak the language of the culture yet confront that culture with the authentic person of Jesus Christ? First we must learn the language of the culture. To learn the language of a culture, we must also love the culture. We must immerse ourselves in the culture. Even as we interrogate and challenge and confront the culture, we must love the world as God has loved the world. We must revel in its beauty and creativity, in its joy and struggles. In this way, we learn the nuances of its language. This is the vibrant intellectual and spiritual activity we must create on our Christian university campuses.

But Newbigin is clear about the other side of this engagement: We must also know what the gospel story has to say. None of this makes sense or will have any compelling urgency unless we as individuals and as Christian communities have encountered the crucified and living Christ. It is that transforming experience with the person of Jesus that makes any of this viable or necessary or urgent. There is no issue here, no purpose, no direction, unless we are driven by the understanding that the gospel of Jesus is the good news for our world. We must establish our fundamental presupposition.

But then, finally, we offer the culture an opportunity to turn from bad news to good news. We offer an *invitation* into the culture to turn back from the way of death and to embrace the good news of human flourishing. And as we both articulate and model this way of living, we trust that our invitation becomes compelling. This is the goal of engaging the culture.

Recently I was speedily driving down the street on my way to some kind of meeting, and I found myself listening to the radio. I had tuned in to one of those talk-radio stations, where mostly political issues are vehemently debated, often in the shrill voices of political divide in which we find ourselves. It was lively, heated, engaging and often polarizing.

The terms of discourse simply shut out any notion that God is important to the issues being discussed. To think that I might hear any meaningful discussion of the power of the gospel in our world—well, I was not holding my breath. As Christians, we have come to expect truncated conversations like these, conversations that leave out what is so truly important to us. We have grown to accept these terms of public discourse.

This talk-radio station is one of the many signals out there that talking about God in public is "problematic," as we say. In fact, in so many

social and business situations, we often go silent about God's importance in our lives, seeking not to offend, seeking not to embarrass ourselves and others. The "pressures of duplicity" for Christians are huge,
says Hunter. So many times we find ourselves "managing our identities" in public. We somehow feel that the "consequence of disclosure"
will drive us from being accepted in places that are important to us.
"The temptation to be deceptive or dishonest [about one's faith] is enormous," Hunter says.[4]

Later that same day I was heading to another destination, and I
switched the dial to what we call Christian radio. There I heard a voice
speaking a language altogether different from the one on the first station. I found lots of conversation about God and faith and the gospel,
but it suddenly dawned on me that this was a language and tone that
seemed to have no overlap with the world of the first station. Indeed,
when there was any mention of the other culture, the posture was one
of confrontation, disdain and dismissal.

My heart grew heavy about all this. The language of the Christian
station is often an insider's language, esoteric and foreign to the ears of
so many who are drawn to public debate. It is truly a foreign language,
a language unintelligible to anyone outside the fold of Christian culture. As Hunter writes, "The grammar of Christian faith has become
more strange and arcane, less natural and more foreign, spoken awk-
wardly if at all. To be sure, 'God-talk' is certainly possible within the
framework of the church, but outside religious community it has little
or no resonance at all."[5]

This is very discouraging. A wide gap has opened up between these
two worlds. We live in a bilingual culture, at best, one public and secular, dominated by the terms that must exclude the language of people of
faith. This is the culture where, as I described earlier, Easter has been
airbrushed off the map. In the other world, we find a language that is
religious but exclusive, dominated by insider-talk that is unintelligible
to the other culture, where most people live. Few of us are adept at
translating between the two. And I believe this gap is damaging to the

---

[4]Hunter, *To Change the World*, pp. 258-59.
[5]Ibid., p. 203.

work of God's people in the world.

I am not suggesting that the Christian radio station adopt the shrill tone of the other, nor that it need alter its subject matter so that all we are listening to is politics or ideology. But somehow, if engaging the culture is our goal as Christians, we must learn the language of the culture so well, and we must learn to translate the gospel so effectively that we find ourselves speaking openly and naturally the good news we want so desperately to share. That is Newbigin's point: We must bring these languages into some sort of healthy interface and do so winsomely. Somehow we must become effective translators across the divide, and I believe the burden for such engagement rests on Christians.

None of this is easy. I often speak to a broad audience in my community, and I am well aware that there is no possible way the usual audience in Seattle is prepared to hear something openly or directly about my Christian story. I have to find a new language to express my faith commitments. I have to be a translator when I speak, or I will jeopardize any hearing at all.

As I step off the platform, I often think, *Oh my, I was too Christian in that one. I hope I have not shut out my audience or alienated someone from listening to what I have to say.* At other times I step away thinking, *Oh my, I was simply not Christian enough. Am I ashamed of the gospel? Do they really know what is so deeply important to me, at the heart and core of my person and my vision for my university?* Speaking into this gap between cultures is hugely challenging, but it is essential if we have any hope to change the world.

N. T. Wright asks, How do we "rightly reappropriate" the gospel "in the world of late modernity, postmodernity, post-colonialism, neo-imperialism, and all the other things that swirl around our heads at the start of the twenty-first century"?[6] This is our challenge—the "challenge of Jesus," to use the title of one of Wright's books. And what an exciting challenge—daunting, frustrating at times, hopeful and yet discouraging, joyous—this is work of engaging the culture, the central

---

[6]N. T. Wright, *Paul: In Fresh Perspective* (Minneapolis: Fortress, 2005), p. 172.

task of the twenty-first-century Christian and indeed central to the work of the Christian university we are trying to imagine for our time.

———————————————— ∎ ————————————————

I am fully aware that not all my friends and colleagues in Christian higher education agree with me on these matters. When I get to waxing passionate about cultural engagement, sometimes eyes glaze over among my colleagues. Many of our Christian institutions, especially the great Christian liberal arts colleges, come out of a tradition that tilts in the direction of separation from culture. Many are in isolated places where connection to our powerful urban centers is limited. We have often structured our institutions so that our students separate from the world "for a time," as we say, so they may then "enter the world" prepared. This is the ivory tower model. This is the belief that there is something called pure learning, that intellectual pursuit is worthy as its own end, even as we saw with John Henry Newman.

But I do not buy into these notions. Such a tradition may have been appropriate for another time, but no longer. It seems abundantly clear that *the gospel calls us into vigorous cultural engagement.* Any preparation apart from this core commitment—to engage the culture—neglects the central call of the gospel on our Christian universities. We must engage the culture to change the world. In my opinion, this is the clear and critical direction for the future of the Christian university.

13

PAUL'S EXPLOSIVE VISION

> *Part of Paul's task, in teaching the Christian hope
> to puzzled converts, was precisely to educate their imagination,
> to lift their eyes beyond the small horizons
> of their previous worldviews.*
>
> N. T. WRIGHT

How THEN DO WE GO ABOUT REBUILDING a Christian university from the inside out, a university that dedicates itself to making the world a better place for all of God's children? We have begun that process by listening to the wise counsel of Lesslie Newbigin about engaging the culture with the gospel of Jesus Christ. This posture of winsome engagement is our starting point.

But we also need to know how we locate the powerful Christian story right at the animating heart of the whole learning enterprise. We want to rebuild trust in the authority of our ancient story, in a day and age when all authority is under attack, a day when suspicion rather than trust is the defining tone our culture encourages us to adopt. We need to understand in fresh new ways that the whole gospel of Jesus calls us to make the world a better place, and then we need to equip ourselves and our students to roll up our sleeves and get on with the work to be done. Let's take the next steps in defining just what this means.

•

Several summers ago I had one of those reading encounters that can change a person's life. Somehow my vision for the work of the Christian university took on a much more expansive scope—through this fresh encounter with the Scriptures. As part of what I had planned for study through that summer season, I opened for a fresh reading Paul's first letter to the Christian church in the secular, urban setting of Corinth. I also carried with me Richard Hays's fine commentary on the letter, intending to do an in-depth reading of text and context, intending to be nourished for my life and work.

I used to tell my students that one good definition of a classic is that it speaks to the reader in each new reading, no matter one's age or circumstance at the moment. And so I turned to this classic text with eager expectation that it would meet me where I lived most intensely, at that moment in my life—because I am one of those peculiar people who marks major turning points in life through an encounter with a powerful text.

The exuberant writer of 1 Corinthians begins his letter this way:

> From Paul, apostle of Christ Jesus by God's call and by his will, together with our colleague Sosthenes, to God's church at Corinth, dedicated to him in Christ Jesus, called to be his people, along with all who invoke the name of our Lord Jesus Christ wherever they may be—their Lord as well as ours. (1 Corinthians 1:1-2)

That's it. That's the opening of this great book, one sentence, a whole two verses in our Bible, a large stack of clauses. But what an opening!

These simple and oh-so-familiar verses blew my mind and my imagination wide open. I know that sounds like an exaggeration, but it's true. Somehow, they powerfully spoke into my reflections about the Christian university, the subject that has occupied so much of my thinking over the years. Somehow these verses framed for me how we might imagine anew our encounter as Christians with secular, urban culture and what the scope of our thinking must be if we have any chance of influencing a chaotic world with the gospel of Jesus Christ. This text taps down into the deep roots of the ancient story, digging down to establish an anchor. And then it imaginatively and expansively reaches out to encompass the whole world.

Perhaps I began to experience in this encounter what Hays calls a "conversion of the imagination." He is talking not just about what happened to Paul on the road to Damascus, but also about the transformation of mind and imagination that began as Paul read the Scriptures *after* his dramatic encounter with our risen Lord. If we watch carefully what happens as Paul reads the Scriptures with new eyes, we find "a way of reading that summons the reader to an epistemological transformation, a conversion of the imagination," says Hays.[1] Wow, imagine that! A whole new way of looking at things, through the very act of reading! Ultimately this conversion calls us to a new way of living, a new vision of our responsibilities in the world. All of this from a new reading of the Scriptures!

If we follow Paul's example of "how to read Scripture faithfully, the church's imagination will be converted to see both Scripture and the world in a radically new way," Hays says.[2] That's the way I want to read Scripture. That's the exciting venture of reading I propose, a venture of interpretation. That's the kind of reading we must imagine at the heart of our work as Christian universities—if we expect the Scriptures to radiate out from the center of who we are as universities.

■

These first two verses of 1 Corinthians are extraordinary: one long, unwieldy sentence, with clause stacked upon clause, building toward an exuberant, highly charged crescendo. This sentence articulates an imaginative vision for this scruffy, scrappy little group of Christians in their bustling, secular urban center of Corinth. This vision is intended literally to lift the church out of its petty squabbles, its dissension and confusion, and to cast for these people a notion that they are part of a huge, unfolding drama all across the world.

Paul wants this gathering of new Christians in Corinth to know that they have joined a movement that is changing the world. He seems to be saying that we are connected to a huge drama going on out there,

---

[1]Richard Hays, *The Conversion of the Imagination: Paul as Interpreter of Israel's Scripture* (Grand Rapids: Eerdmans, 2005), p. x.
[2]Ibid., p. viii.

God's drama, a drama unfolding as we speak. This drama is spreading the good news of the new gospel all over the world. It is unified by the power of Jesus Christ to change people's live—no doubt about it. So there is a center! And we need to understand that this good news is not for us alone. We have a chance to bring the light of that gospel into the world so that all of God's children might flourish. Imagine that!

These sentences contain just this kind of enthusiasm and exuberance. This venture is exciting, exhilarating.

——————————————————— ▪ ———————————————————

Paul begins this long sentence by announcing his calling, as he usually does in his letters: he is writing as an "apostle of Christ Jesus by God's call and by his will." He feels the need to affirm and assert his authority for the writing of this letter. He is establishing his credentials, his credibility. It seems clear throughout the letter that authority and credibility are part of the debate going on in the Corinthian church, as in our own day. There seems to be a crisis of authority, to use Hannah Arendt's language about our own time.

Whom shall we trust as the authentic interpreter of the ancient Scriptures, the Jews were asking with urgency after the appearance of Jesus. How do we know who has the right angle on these weighty questions unfolding out of our long tradition and teaching? In this pluralist, relativist Corinthian culture in which we live, how do we know which story about Jesus presents to us what is true and good and beautiful? We seem to be living in a world of colliding maps. Who's to say what story is true?

Of course the question of authority is focused on Paul's reading of the Scriptures. To find in Jesus the ultimate fulfillment of the long-promised Messiah; to realize that in this Jesus we now finally can break out of the confinement and limitations of our ethnicity and spread God's light to the whole world—this was the radical new reading of Scripture that Paul is announcing. That the church is actually fulfilling God's ancient promise to Abraham that his people will be a light for the whole world—to make such expansive, life-changing, world-changing assertions—Paul knows he must speak with authority. He knows he will be met with suspicion, but he also knows for certain that authority is always the question when you are proposing and promoting a radical shift in the way people look at the world.

Paul's new claim is really one of how to read Scripture. His personal, transforming encounter with the risen Jesus on that fateful journey to Damascus turned his attention immediately and imaginatively to the reinterpretation of Scripture. And that is always a powerful combination, isn't it? An encounter with Jesus and the subsequent rereading of Scriptures. This was not a leap into another drama, another story, but a reinterpretation of the grand narrative in which Paul was living. It is a big and long drama, he knows and so passionately believes. It is God's drama from the beginning of time. The thing that has radically changed is that God's promises, out of the deep roots of scriptural tradition, are now seen with new eyes in the light of Jesus. And now the task is to devote ourselves both to new reading and to new action.

And then comes the vision so full of imaginative possibilities: you are "called to be his people" (what energy and exuberance and empowerment lies in that phrase!); people of mixed ethnicities and backgrounds (the radical reconciliation that takes place in this vision is astounding); in fact, you are called "along with all who invoke the name of our Lord Jesus Christ" (this is now where the transformed imagination begins to take hold, because once again we are joined together in Christ—"*all* who invoke the name") "wherever they may be—their Lord as well as ours."

"Wherever they may be"—Paul's imagination has exploded out of the fixed boundaries with new possibilities—all across the globe, breaking the confinement and restriction of his own ethnicity as a Jew, a message of hope and good news to all of God's children all over the globe, "wherever they may be." We are in the rhetorical hands of no small thinker. This is not a small imagination we are encountering here. This is huge. This is a vision to change the world.

"Something has happened," Paul seems to be telling his readers. "There is a big movement out there. You Corinthians have written to me about some of your confusion regarding appropriate Christian behavior and your constant bickering among yourselves about who's the real leader for the new way. You have even questioned my authority. You have told me about the culture in which you are trying to live out this new message, a culture that marginalizes the core of the gospel. And you have expressed your frustration that the 'word of the cross' is such foolishness to the broader culture, and really a scandal to the Jewish community. All of this is important, but listen: It all fits only into the context of this global movement of God's vision for human flourishing as found in Jesus Christ." Catch the vision, Paul seems to be saying. Join the team. We have a chance to change the world with this new way of Jesus Christ!

After this powerful opening vision, the text takes an abrupt shift. In verse 10, Paul begins to talk about what we would call Christian community formation. He has just communicated his vision for the world, and now he says it all must begin at home. He says, "I appeal to you, my friends, in the name of our Lord Jesus Christ" (once again establishing the grounding in Christ) "agree among yourselves and avoid divisions; let there be complete unity of mind and thought." In essence, he is saying "stop fighting with one another! We've got work to do." Come together for the grand work to which we are called. All this bickering and fighting contributes to a squandering of our extraordinary opportunity to shape the culture and change the world. We simply cannot let ourselves get caught up in this polarizing and paralyzing dividedness and divisiveness. The stakes are too high to be focusing on ourselves.

Oh my, what a charge! A charge that has been violated across the span of Christian history. Lives have been lost in violation of this strong and clear admonition to marshal our energies *in unity*, to come together in love and community, to show the world that Christians do things radically differently. As part of the mission of my university, Seattle Pacific University, we have declared that we will seek to "model grace-filled community and practice radical reconciliation." In the beginning of my work, I realized we were a group of Christians who had grown politicized and divided, as so many universities are; we were bickering and adversarial. I began to try to encourage us all toward "grace-filled community," a commitment that must be part of our core values, the way we do business. This language was eventually adopted in our mission statement.

I have always felt that as the world looks in on our work as a Christian university, looks in on the way we do our business, people should be able to see something radically different, something quite countercultural. They should be able to look in and say, "These people know how to get along." What a powerful model that can change the world!

In 1 Corinthians 13, Paul wrote some of the most extraordinary words on love in all human literature. Though this text is most often assigned to wedding ceremonies, I propose it is not about love between a man and a woman, though it can be about that as well. Rather it is about how to live in community. Love is the glue. Love is the grounding, the unifying energy. Love is the connecting tissue that keeps us whole. And this is the only way we can effectively translate and communicate the gospel into the world we seek to change. To Paul, "the imperative of the gospel meant, above all, unity," N. T. Wright says.[3] Given the vision that we are called to change the world, we must begin at home, where love and grace-filled community are the way we do business as a university.

Finally, Paul comes to the most compelling and challenging part of the vision. He shifts gears again and says that God has called him "to proclaim the gospel; and to do it without recourse to the skills of rhetoric, lest the cross of Christ be robbed of its effect" (1 Corinthians 1:17). Now, what is this all about? What is Paul adding to the equation, to this grand vision, with this talk about the "cross of Christ"?

We have hit the mother lode of the gospel for Paul in 1 Corinthians. The cross is at the heart of it all, and lest we forget, this "message of the cross is sheer folly" to most of the world, most certainly to the culture in which we do our work (1 Corinthians 1:18). It is indeed a scandal, not only to the Jews of Paul's day but also to Christians in our own time.

---

[3]N. T. Wright, *Paul: In Fresh Perspective* (Minneapolis: Fortress, 2005), p. 165.

We can imagine the Christians at Corinth asking, as we all ask, What in the world are you talking about? How are we expected to bring good news if the cross is what defines our very identity and binds us together in Christian community? It is most certainly, Paul says, a scandal to the Jews and foolishness to the Greeks, so why in the world would we ever think to lift high the cross of Jesus? "Christ nailed to the cross"—this is the "power of God and the wisdom of God"—really? (1 Corinthians 1:22-24). Paul was even fully aware that to translate the message of the cross into the culture was an enormous challenge, even dangerous—as it is today, of course—but absolutely essential.

Paul has some stern talk about the "wisdom of this world," which will always find itself in opposition to this "message of the cross." This powerful and wise word of the cross is "not a wisdom belonging to this present age or to its governing powers." Indeed, we each "must become a fool" if we want "to be truly wise" (1 Corinthians 2:6; 3:18). Now there's a challenge for those of us who labor to bring distinction to our universities: How do we make sense of such advice?

Even though Paul assures his listeners that the powers of this day are "already in decline" and that those who live by the wisdom of the cross will in the end "overthrow the existing order," we are hard pressed to understand (1 Corinthians 2:6). We are not convinced.

Some time ago, my wife and I attended one of the historic, tall-steeple, evangelical churches in Southern California, Hollywood Presbyterian Church. We were vacationing with our family in Pasadena and went to church with our son and daughter-in-law, who attended there.

Hollywood Presbyterian Church has a legacy of audaciously thriving right in the heart of the movie capital of the world, that powerful shaper of the culture. It is the home of the legendary Henrietta Mears, sometimes known as the mother of Sunday school, an extraordinary Bible teacher and mentor to many future leaders in the evangelical Presbyterian church. Mears's tradition of strong biblical teaching and vigorous understanding of the surrounding culture is carried on to this day in the weekly teaching at Hollywood Presbyterian by my dear friend Dale Bruner, a superb Bible teacher.

As we came to church that morning, we had heard the stories that the church was deeply hurting, splintered over very serious management issues. People were fighting and angry, we were told, and fiercely questioning the credibility and authority of leaders in the church. Those who still attended the church were bitter, hurt and disappointed. They felt betrayed by their leaders. The church's congregational meetings were apparently nasty and vicious. Not a pretty picture—but neither was the situation at Paul's Corinthian church.

On the Sunday that we visited, Lloyd Ogilvie returned to the pulpit as guest preacher. Lloyd was the pastor at Hollywood Presbyterian for many years and went on to become the chaplain of the U. S. Senate. When Lloyd stood up to speak, the congregation rose to its feet in thunderous applause. This was their leader of old, in the days when they were held together in unity and Christian community. The applause surely expressed a yearning to be restored, for unity of mind and purpose, the kind of unity Paul encourages. Maybe their former pastor could help. Maybe he could bring healing and harmony and peace. Maybe Lloyd could bring them together so they could continue to engage the culture with the gospel and bring the good news into the Hollywood community once again.

Would Lloyd enter into the fray of their church politics? Would he choose sides? Did he have some worldly wisdom to offer them, some wisdom he had gained in the halls of the Senate, something that might bring healing and reconciliation to the dividedness in which they were so painfully entangled?

Well, Lloyd began his sermon by talking about a day in the eighties— the day a huge, sculpted stone cross would be set in place on top of the church. Everyone on the church staff gathered out on the walk to witness this new and wonderful addition to the church, Lloyd said. The cranes arrived. Some who were driving or walking by stopped to watch. The big cross was lifted up into the sky and secured on the pinnacle of the church so that everyone in Hollywood, everyone driving down "the 101"—the historic Hollywood Freeway—could see that this church gathered beneath the cross of Jesus. Hollywood Presbyterian had its cross, a symbol of the grand story that could change lives and change the world, a cross that would challenge the wisdom of the world.

Then Lloyd came to his point that morning and said something like this: "Since that day, when we hoisted the big stone cross on the top of our church, I have imagined that this great church gathers each week right here under the cross. We do the work of the church beneath the cross of Jesus. And for the world we lift high the cross of Christ. And this is a moment in the life of this church to come again to the foot of the cross. With all of our anger and bitterness and hurt, our confusion and our sense of betrayal, let us bring it all right here and lay it at the foot of the cross. Because only there will we know healing and unity again."

Lloyd was asking the congregation to think clearly that, as the great stone cross still sits on top of the church, the world looks in to see what wisdom Hollywood Presbyterian lives by and how they do the work of the church—there under this cross of Jesus. What kind of people live under a cross? Well, they live in unity and love and respect for each other. They treat each other with kindness and civility. They carry a good word—good news—out into the streets of Hollywood. And they avoid the easy indulgence of the bad news of dividedness and divisiveness. They are not, like the rest of the world, trapped in suspicion, disrespect, incivility and broken trust. When we remember what Paul means by the wisdom of the word of the cross, our own wounds will be healed. This is the only way we can carry the good news out into the world.

Paul makes a strong assertion about the word of the cross: It is a call to humility and gratitude. Live with humility, as Jesus modeled for us, humility that calls us to the supreme sacrifice he made on the cross. Live with gratitude for what he has done, for new life, for the light of the world that lives beyond death in the resurrection, for wholeness and healing, even in the midst of a broken and hurting world. Living in humility and gratitude is a tall order in our world today. Living under the cross is an act of foolishness to the world.

But this, Paul says, is our power to change the world. If we are to be effective as we take the good news of the gospel through our very enterprise as universities and spread it out into the world, we must let that profound and powerful word of the cross sit right at the center of who we are. We must carry ourselves with humility and gratitude. We must be transformed by the cross. Our imagination must be radically changed to imagine another way of living in community.

——————————————— ▪ ———————————————

N. T. Wright says that Paul calls us to reconstruct the self and reconstruct our very way of knowing. This comes through

> the reconstruction of the great story. The grand narrative of modernity, of progress and Enlightenment, has run out of steam in most areas. . . . With it, all grand narratives have been seen as exploitative, as power-plays, as attempts to snatch the high ground and rule other stories out of consideration. But, once more, the story which Paul tells, and equally importantly the story he lived out day by day, is a story not of power but of love. There is, of course, a power which comes with that, but it is made perfect only in weakness. The paradox of the cross is the great theme of the new grand story, preventing it ever—if it is true to itself—from being twisted by knaves to make a trap for fools.[4]

This "paradox of the cross" must be the beginning point as we seek to describe the Christian university for our time, an enterprise sketched out by the imagination, an enterprise of learning and action that is shaped daily by embracing the ancient Christian story. We embrace a story that calls us, even as a university, to commit ourselves to grace-filled community, radical reconciliation and unity of purpose. Ours must be a community that finds its identity beneath the cross of Jesus Christ. In gratitude and humility, we are charged to bring this story of what is true and good and beautiful, a good-news story, into all the world, to all of God's children. Our reach can be nothing short of astounding, a drama that goes on all across the globe in a movement we are privileged to join.

Wright says that "part of Paul's task, in teaching the Christian hope

---

[4]Ibid., pp. 173-74.

to puzzled converts, was precisely to educate their imagination, to lift their eyes beyond the small horizons of their previous worldviews."[5] Our job as Christians in a postmodern world and as Christian universities in a post-Christian world is to teach Christian hope and joy and radiance. We must lift our eyes "beyond the small horizons" of our self-limiting view of the power of the gospel.

The vision is expansive. The opportunities are huge. And the world is ripe and hungry for change. This is the territory in which we go to work as Christian universities for our day. This is why our universities stand the chance of being the place where world change begins.

---

[5]Ibid., p. 130.

14

RESTORING COMMUNITIES OF TRUST

Living as we do on this side of the Enlightenment,
we cannot escape the intellectual impact of the great "masters
of suspicion": Nietzsche, Marx, Freud, and more recently Foucault,
along with other purveyors of "critical theory."

RICHARD HAYS

The larger goal is not simply to produce critical thinkers,
but to equip persons who are faithful to the truth of the gospel.
Some of us must engage in critical thinking in order
to be effective in encouraging God's people to be faithful,
both to the biblical message and to all that is good and worthy
in the Christian traditions that we have received.

RICHARD MOUW

ONE OF THE MOST URGENT NEEDS OF OUR day is to build new
communities of trust. We must model trusting relationships. Trust
matters. And restoring a culture of trust is critical to our venture of
changing the world. We will not flourish without trust.

Trust must be earned. It takes time and perseverance and discipline
to build trust. Trust also must be given: we must learn how to carry
ourselves trustingly. This is complicated business, I know, and I have
no illusions that the task ahead will be easy.

So, what are the challenges and obstacles that lie before us as we seek to build communities of trust? For more than a century, we have been guided in our culture by the "masters of suspicion," as Richard Hays calls them: Nietzsche, Marx, Freud, Foucault, and so many others. We have absorbed this teaching of suspicion, whether we have studied these "masters" or not.

It is not just in the intellectual and academic world where we get this message. I recently saw an advertising banner wrapped around the tail of a bus. Two local news anchors were trumpeted there as "professional skeptics." This was meant to be appealing, I suppose—this hip TV station is coming to my rescue by providing professional skepticism about almost anything. As we read our papers each morning and listen to our news each evening, adopting this posture of suspicion becomes as natural as drinking our coffee. We drink in skepticism, lack of trust, suspicion—even cynicism—without even knowing we are doing so.

Our students come into our universities having already adopted our culture's posture of suspicion. And, of course, our universities actually encourage such a posture. I recently sat at breakfast with the president of one of the major universities in the Northeast. He announced proudly that he tells his students, "It is the job of this university to provide you with a strong, life-long attitude of suspicion toward all authority."

In his book *The Age of Turbulence*, Alan Greenspan, longtime chair of the Federal Reserve, focuses on the fundamental need for trust if we are to have a healthy economy. He makes the point that the market economy will flourish only when it operates within a culture of trust. When trust is broken badly and distrust is pervasive, as we have seen in recent decades, the economy falters and ultimately collapses.

As the societies and economies of the Soviet Union were breaking out from under iron-fisted control, Russians, along with millions of people in Eastern Europe, had to rediscover how to "trust in the word of others, especially strangers," Greenspan says. Trust was "conspicuously lacking in the new Russia."[1] One could not trust the government

[1]Alan Greenspan, *The Age of Turbulence: Adventures in a New World* (New York: Penguin Press, 2007), p. 140.

to be truthful. Betrayal of trust penetrated into everyday life, so that people could not trust their neighbors. Even family members were not beyond suspicion. Trust had been buried deeply in a culture of lies. No healthy economy can function in such a world. The economic recovery of Russia, still unfolding as I write, was profoundly hindered by this culture of deep suspicion, sharpened and developed over decades of brutish repression and broken trust.

We learned the same thing in America during the business scandals of the Enron era and beyond. We too have developed a culture of suspicion out of pervasive patterns of betrayal. We continue to learn about the consequences of broken trust in the still-unfolding story of the credit crisis of 2008. I think here especially of the collapse of massive financial schemes like the one constructed over decades by Bernie Madoff. Without the chilling betrayal of simple human trust, that sixty-five-billion-dollar house of cards could not have been built. In business and economic terms, as Greenspan says, "trust has to be earned; reputation is often the most valuable asset a business has," and when trust is violated, something vital to our economy and our society is lost.[2] Broken trust tears at the fabric of our society, our culture and our relationships. Once broken, trust is so very hard to restore.

■

In Dante's powerful and haunting work *The Inferno*, written in the early fourteenth century, those who betrayed the trust of others were located in the Ninth Circle of hell, down "at the bottom of the universe." As we take Dante's horrifying journey through hell, on our way down to that bottom, we have already passed those who are consumed with lust (now endlessly tossed about by wind), down past the gluttons, past those who are controlled by anger, past the heretics, past even the violent. But down there "beyond all others ill-begot," says Dante, the Ninth Circle is the eternal home for the *betrayers*, the ones who violate trust.[3]

[2]Ibid., p. 141.
[3]Dante, *Inferno*, canto 34, st. 19.

Because their hearts grew cold through lives of betraying, they were encased in ice; only their eyes are visible above the surface. This is the Circle of Cain and Brutus and, worst of all, Judas. The head of Judas is lodged between the fangs of Lucifer, and Lucifer's claws "sliced / And tore the skin until his back was stripped."[4] This goes on daily, eternally. This is the fate of the betrayers. Dante believed that betrayal, the breaking of trust, was the most egregious and destructive violation within the human community.

We know how harmful the consequences of betrayal are. If we are going to have a flourishing society, we must educate for trust, not suspicion. We must work to restore communities of trust that model another way of living in human community.

——————————————— ▪ ———————————————

Let's think here for a moment about the phenomenon surrounding the publication of Dan Brown's *The Da Vinci Code*. The primary proposition of this novel is that we cannot trust the historic sources of Christian Scripture or tradition. This book comes straight out of the culture of suspicion we have been talking about, demonstrating for us confusion within our culture about authority. It poses as the bearer of big news: we simply cannot trust the root sources of the ancient Christian story. It is a fraud, we are told. "If you know what I know," the writer seems to be saying, "you will never trust the promises of the gospel of Jesus ever again. That story is no longer credible. It is just another good story bumping around in the universe of meaning, to be accepted or denied as you please."

Such a challenge is fair enough. Christians must always be willing to stand up when the sources of our faith are challenged. We must be willing, as the apostle Peter says, to make the case for the hope we find within us (1 Peter 3:15). Trust must be built on solid ground, on clear, critical thinking. We trust the sources of our story by faith ultimately, but also by good thinking throughout the ages, by hard and faithful

---

[4]Ibid.

attention to the details of our story, by strong historical research, by interpretative sophistication.

What I find so remarkable, even quite astounding, about the conversation surrounding *The Da Vinci Code* is the question of *authority*. Who says the story of Jesus is true? And who says the story is not true? Who says the story of the early centuries of our faith tradition is something completely other than what we have been told? Where does such authority come from? Who gives Dan Brown such authority to mount the challenges he does? How can we, in our culture of suspicion, answer these questions?

The gritty early-twentieth-century journalist H. L. Mencken famously said that a Puritan is one who lies awake at night with the haunting fear that someone, somewhere, is having fun. As I go about mounting a challenge to some of the misguided assumptions of *The Da Vinci Code*, and especially as I reflect on the cultural phenomenon stirred up by this book, I find myself muttering, "Oh come on now. The whole thing is nothing more than a good read, a thriller. Don't be so sensitive, so defensive." Ron Howard, the director of the movie based on the book, chastens with a similar sentiment: "It's not history, and it's not theology; instead, it's just a rollicking good bit of entertainment." I have no desire to try to rain on such a parade of good fun. I enjoyed the novel too. And besides, Lord save us from dour Puritanism.

But in an interview with Matt Lauer on the *Today Show*, Brown said nonchalantly that "all of it is based on historic fact." There is that magic word—*fact*—so often used to make a clear demarcation between what we know by the facts and what we presume to know by faith. Brown is consistently portrayed by the media and by his own self-promotion as a thorough and meticulous researcher. "The only things fictional in the book are the characters," Brown said to Linda Wertheimer on National Public Radio. "Everything else is factual."

Apparently Brown wants to portray the movie as more than "just a rollicking good bit of entertainment." He wants to propose that we are about to encounter the *truthful* retelling of the Christian story. "Let me tell you what really happened," he seems to say between every line. "And watch out, there may be some shocking new angles that will liberate us all from two thousand years of damaging illusion. You will now have the facts, the long kept secret, with which to decide whether Jesus is who he said he was and whether the Christian Scriptures have any validity at all."

The novel, for example, presents as *fact* that Jesus was married to Mary Magdalene and that, as he hung on the cross, Mary was carrying their child. Have you ever thought about that one? We discover along the way that their progeny still live in France and that all this information has been kept secret for these two thousand years, suppressed by a male-dominated church so women could not have their rightful power in the Christian movement. "Well," the author seems to be saying, "do I have your attention yet? Has my suspicion opened up for you a can of worms you would rather not see? Isn't my act of breaking your trust in these simple and ancient stories a good thing for you in the long run? Let's get rid of all this nonsense, because that is precisely what it is."

Jesus is just another teacher, so the story goes. This is a Jesus now finally squared with our postmodern concerns that we should not claim too much to be true. Be careful of claims that this self-proclaimed Son of God might be something special, claims that he was in fact the long-awaited Messiah of Jewish history and Scripture, claims that emerged out of God's grand promise to make things right in the end, claims that he died and rose from the grave to launch a totally new way of seeing things. Well, all of this was nothing more than mere fiction, the novel suggests, cooked up by a bunch of guys in the early church who wanted power. In fact, Jesus was a fraud, this new, self-appointed authority proclaims. The Christian Scriptures are all distortions—and the cover-up continues to this day. Those are the "facts," we are led to believe.

The first word in the book is *fact*, implying that what we are about to experience is based on fact. Brown claims on this page, for example, that descriptions about a mysterious secret society called the Priory of Sion are fact. In addition, at an even simpler level, he touts sophisticated accuracy in his descriptions of architecture, detail that does indeed provide some of the delight and texture of the novel. But can we go along with the author that we are entering the realm of fact and accuracy? Can we rely on his authority?

N. T. Wright says that the stories about the Priory of Sion are "really forgeries cooked up by three zany Frenchmen in the 1950s. They cheerfully confessed to this in a devastating television program shown on British television." He notes quite playfully that the "accurate" descriptions of Westminster Abbey, for example, are blatantly distorted and could have been corrected with a ten-minute walk through this glorious structure.[5] Wright should know. He occupied an office as canon theologian at Westminster for a number of years.

Wright asks, "If Brown is so careless, and carelessly inventive, in details as easy to check as those, why should we trust him in anything else?" Wright says quite emphatically that "the deepest irony is that [*The Da Vinci Code*] portrays itself as historically rooted, when it is a tissue of fantasy." He adds, "Any picture of Jesus . . . [must] be produced by serious and sober historical scholarship."[6]

Brown has cobbled together some bits and pieces from the Gnostic texts unearthed in 1945 in the desert of upper Egypt. This was an extraordinary discovery, called Nag Hammadi. He believes, contrary to a significant body of scholarship, that these texts destroy the creditability of the New Testament canon. He also presents as fact a misunderstanding of what happened at the First Council of Nicaea in 325, where he supposes that Constantine suppressed the real truth to solidify power.

The historical sequence presented by Brown is also out of whack. The texts he honors come centuries after Christ, and the record is entirely silent on some of Brown's key assumptions. The real story, by the way, is as intriguing and intellectually exciting as anything presented in the novel. According to New Testament scholar Ben Witherington, Brown's argument, like so many others in this vein, is based on a record of silence, and "in the end, we still have to make arguments based on history, not on silence." The argument of Brown and others to "attempt to show that the process of forming the New Testament was somehow arbitrary and manipulative is a failure, and it seems to be driven by

---

[5]N. T. Wright, "Decoding *The Da Vinci Code*," address delivered at Seattle Pacific University for the President's Symposium on the Gospel and Cultural Engagement, Seattle, WA, May 18-19, 2005.
[6]Ibid.

something other than historical scholarship."[7]

Hannah Arendt suggested that the Western world was suffering from a "crisis of authority" already in the mid-twentieth century. Who's to say what is fact and what is fiction? Truth according to whom? And isn't history all a matter of how you read it and who is doing the reading? In such a time as this, we do indeed begin to select our "teachers to suit our own likings," as the apostle Paul cautioned Timothy in the first-century church (2 Timothy 4:3). How we answer these questions about authority is as important as anything we can do as Christian universities. How we settle the question of trust is profoundly important for the future of our world.

——————————————— ■ ———————————————

As Paul spoke into the culture of his own day, he called both Jews and Greeks to trust the Scriptures. He called them to see that the radical fulfillment of the Scriptures occurred in the death and resurrection of Jesus. This trust, then, led to a "sweeping reevaluation of their identities, an imaginative paradigm shift so comprehensive that it can only be described as a 'conversion of the imagination,'" Richard Hays says.[8] This conversion comes only out of trust. There can be no change of this sweeping sort, a "reevaluation" of our very "identities," without trust, without reading the Scriptures trustingly. This is what it means to be "hermeneutically reconfigured by the cross and the resurrection." This is what it means to have a "hermeneutics of trust." To be sure, this is a "complex imaginative act,"[9] but just as surely it is the territory into which we must enter as Christians. I submit this is the work of the Christian university for our time.

But how do we go about restoring trust when we live in a culture that chooses to accept the authority of something like *The Da Vinci Code*? Millions of people are willing to swallow anything, no matter how

---

[7]Ben Witherington III, "Why 'The Lost Gospels' Lost Out," *Christianity Today*, June 2004, p. 32.

[8]Richard Hays, *The Conversion of the Imagination: Paul as Interpreter of Israel's Scripture* (Grand Rapids: Eerdmans, 2005), pp. 5-6.

[9]Ibid., p. 11.

flimsy, simply because it seems to offer an alternative to previously authoritative tradition. Our culture revels in the collision of competing maps, where there is no basis, no set of standards, by which to determine the veracity of any one map. How can we trust any map of understanding in such a cultural moment?

——————————————— ▪ ———————————————

Richard Mouw, the president of Fuller Theological Seminary and a thoughtful observer of culture, recently talked about our strong commitment in education to critical thinking: "Are we educating men and women to be critical thinkers? Well, yes, of course." Who among us as educators would ever say we do not need to continue to promote critical thinking? And Lord knows there are students who come to us in our universities and seminaries unable to marshal an argument or to open a text for deeper understanding or to make choices for themselves among many opinions and assertions. Learning critical thinking should be part of any student's intellectual formation.

"But the critical thinking thing must be a moment—a necessary exercise—in the service of a larger process," Mouw says.

> And the larger goal is not simply to produce critical thinkers, but to equip persons who are faithful to the truth of the gospel. Some of us must engage in critical thinking in order to be effective in encouraging God's people to be faithful, both to the biblical message and to all that is good and worthy in the Christian traditions that we have received.[10]

We need critical thinkers for our society to flourish. This is a competency we must provide for our students. But our powerful culture of suspicion can easily lead us to suppose that critical thinking is the end goal of education. Once we have equipped our students with critical thinking, we might think our job is done.

But along with critical thinking, we must reach that "larger goal" of affirming—of trusting—our Christian story. We must renew our com-

---

[10]Richard Mouw, "Critical Thinking," Fuller Theological Seminary President's Blog, June 18, 2007.

mitment to educate for trust. We must learn how to embrace our Christian story *trustingly*. We must learn to read our Scriptures, our own story, trustingly. We must model new communities of trust. This is a radical task for the Christian university of our day. This is the way we will begin to change the world.

15

EMBRACING THE CHRISTIAN STORY

*[Paul] employs Scripture as the source of the world story
in which the community of Christ's people
is to find its identity. This scripturally grounded identity
then shapes the community's action in highly specific ways.*

RICHARD HAYS

*Our distinct impression is that very many religious congregations
and communities of faith in the United States are failing
rather badly in religiously engaging and educating their youth.*

CHRISTIAN SMITH

WE BEGAN OUR DISCUSSION OF THE university of our day by exploring Chaim Potok's vivid metaphor of a world of colliding maps. This metaphor describes quite sharply what it means to live in a postmodern world where there is no larger narrative to guide our thinking or our actions. But Potok said something else very important as he talked about the world of colliding maps. He encouraged our students "to get to know your own map really well."

Study your own map. Know where true north is. Know how your map was drawn. Know where the hills and valleys lie. Try to imagine what's over the horizon. And, above all, do the hard thinking to make sure that your map squares with something real, even if what's real must be accepted trustingly, by faith.

And then there was another suggestion coming through Potok's comments: Despite the intense focus on the individual within the culture, all of this careful study of our own maps must be done in a community of faith and trust.

In Potok's novel *The Gift of Asher Lev*, the main character is both attracted and repelled by the tight Hasidic Jewish community of his family. Asher's people are good to him, though certainly wary of his craft and his success as a world-renowned artist. Their lives are shaped by convictions of strong family and deep community, and this is appealing to Asher. They earnestly worship God together, and though their separatism is strong, they want to shed light for a better way of living into the broader urban community that surrounds them.

Most of all, as believing Jews, they are a people of the Book, a people drawn to the center of their community by the mystery and power of their holy text. "The fire of Torah burns" within them.[1] They embrace their sacred text as the source, as the guide for their lives, as the very reason for being a people called by God to live out his grand drama in the world. They are highly intentional and disciplined in the study of their scriptures. Through long training in their schools and through respected teachers, scholars and authorities, their theological understanding is of the highest sort.

The central tension of the novel comes into focus when Asher is drawn powerfully into the circle of Torah. Toward the end of the novel, on an ordinary Sabbath evening, Asher and his son, Avrumel, head off to the synagogue for Sabbath service. At a key moment in the service, the rhythmic music begins, and the holy text, the scroll of Torah, is brought out onto the floor where all the men are gathered. Suddenly, in the midst of their ecstatic dance, someone thrusts the scroll into Asher's arms. Here is this avatar of individual freedom, this artist who must fiercely guard his creative freedom, holding the ancient text. What will he do with this Torah that has guided and nurtured his community for thousands of years? How is he supposed to participate in this dance of community, this ecstatic gathering, de-

---

[1]Chaim Potok, *The Gift of Asher Lev* (New York: Ballantine Books, 1990), p. 21.

signed over the centuries to draw the community into a circle of meaning around this very text? If he embraces the scroll with abandon, will he give up his freedom to create, the very life blood of his own individual identity?

Asher begins to dance. "I held the scroll," he says,

> as something precious to me, a living being with whose soul I was forever bound, this Sacred Scroll, this Word, this Fire of God, this Source for my own creation, this velvet-encased Fountain of All Life which I now clasped in a passionate embrace. I danced with the Torah for a long time, following the line of dancers through the steamy air of the synagogue and out into the chill tumultuous street and back into the synagogue and then reluctantly yielding the scroll to a huge dark-bearded man, who hungrily scooped it up and swept away with it in his arms.[2]

This is the Jewish love for Torah. This is the deep love expressed throughout the Psalms. This is the love that has held the Jewish community together in meaningful embrace for three thousand years and more. The text is everything to them, surrounded as they are, and always have been, by a hostile secular city. The text is their story, their bigger meaning. It is their very identity as a community in exile. It defines who they are and how they should live. It defines how they should engage their surrounding community, how they should understand the events of the world. Without it, they will lose their bearings in this secular city, and they fiercely, intensely, joyfully hold the text to the center of their lives and their community.

Can we imagine such a dance of joy and love with the Christian Scriptures at the center of our gatherings in Christian community? Can we both literally and figuratively embrace our holy text? It is hard to imagine ourselves so visibly and publicly expressing respect and love for our holy Scriptures. Even if most of us in the Protestant community *weren't* dance-challenged, we are still hard-pressed to see ourselves in such wholehearted embrace of the text of our faith community. I have a hard time imagining Christians shedding our

---

[2]Ibid., p. 362.

posture of cool suspicion about emotion, our hip protective shields of individual freedom, our deep distaste for community rituals that might smother us. I can't imagine rising above our deep fear of anything that restricts our individual freedom and creativity. Even though such an embrace is biblical, we have a hard time yielding—surrendering—to community around the text that defines our identity as followers of Christ.

While our goal should not be to replicate the Jewish ritual, of course, something like it must happen for our Christian communities to be formed and shaped by our sacred, holy, transforming text. Think about this dance in our Christian universities. What would it look like? Some such ritual of respect for our Scriptures might focus and energize the animating center of our learning.

News broke out from Nickel Mines, Pennsylvania, on October 2, 2006, that a mad milk truck driver had barged into a one-room schoolhouse and brutally snuffed out the lives of five little Amish girls. How can we ever make sense of such senseless actions? How is it possible for an individual to proclaim for himself such power and authority over the sacred dignity of the lives of others, especially the lives of children?

Just as puzzling for me was the extraordinary response of the Amish community over the days that followed this heinous act of violence. It is almost impossible for us to make sense, living in our own culture, of the extravagant acts of forgiveness and reconciliation coming out of the Amish community. Perhaps the only way is to surmise that this culture within our culture has been shaped by the Christian Scriptures.

I understand that about half of the mourners who attended the funeral of the killer—a man who somehow thought the wrongs in his past justified his horrific actions against these children—were Amish. The fathers and mothers, the uncles and aunts and cousins, the friends and playmates of the girls—all came to mourn the death of the killer.

The Amish have apparently shaped a profoundly different kind of human community. I'm not talking about the buggies or the kerosene lanterns or the disdain of buttons. Rather, the Scriptures have apparently penetrated this unusual community with values we all deem admirable. It is clear from their actions that over the centuries these people have read the Scriptures with great care and attentiveness. They have embraced the radical Christian story with results that are very different from the surrounding culture.

My wife and I had the privilege one fall evening to visit the home of an Amish family. They had invited a group of Christian university presidents to dinner, an unusual invitation for such outsiders we were told. Before we could eat their hearty Pennsylvania dinner, we sang a hymn, read the Scriptures and prayed together—a good lot of it in Pennsylvania Dutch, an American form of German. I imagined such a ritual, such teaching, happening every evening for hundreds of years. And I thought, *This culture is shaped by this little dinner-time ritual.* This is the way the Christian community has operated throughout history, this gathering around a meal, but gathering first around the holy text that speaks the language of God.

After those Amish girls were shot, it was reported that the oldest girl in the schoolroom, her feet bound by wire and plastic along with the others, asked to be shot first so the other girls might be spared. These were kids who had never seen a movie made in our violence-soaked culture. Judging from the gear their killer brought into their schoolhouse, it is clear that he knew well the ways of vengeance and violence so prevalent in our movies.

Sometimes it takes someone outside the dominant culture to jolt us into seeing how destructive, damaging and degrading our assumptions can be. Mother Teresa comes to mind, she who welcomed the utterly rejected into human community. It was she too who violated all the norms of political correctness by speaking forcefully for the sanctity of the unborn to then President Clinton and other dignitaries at the President's Prayer Breakfast in Washington, D.C. Rosa Parks emphatically took action, convinced that all of God's children deserve a place on the bus. John Paul II announced "the splendor of truth" to a world fiercely suspicious of any notion of truth. Each acted and spoke out of a community of faith anchored and animated by holy Scripture.

———————————— ■ ————————————

Surely the Amish community of Nickel Mines had read many times from Romans 12: "Let hope keep you joyful; in trouble stand firm; persist in prayer; contribute to the needs of God's people, and practice hospitality." We might imagine, for centuries, the high rhythms of Scripture coming out of their farmhouses, saying, "Call down blessings on your persecutors—blessings, not curses. Rejoice with those who rejoice, weep with those who weep. Live in agreement with one another. Do not be proud. . . . Do not keep thinking how wise you are. . . . If possible, so far as it lies with you, live at peace with all" (Romans 12:12-18).

In the 1985 movie *The Witness*, the main character, Detective John Book, played by Harrison Ford, goes into hiding to protect himself and an Amish boy who witnessed a murder. The boy's Amish community takes Book in, without questions, to give him time and space to heal from his wounds. In part because he falls in love with the boy's mother, in part because he is puzzled by the grace with which they take him in, the Ford character ponders the crossings, even the collision, between radically different cultures. He watches the Amish ways, intrigued, full of curiosity, admiring but skeptical. Could he ever leave his own culture and join the Amish? Could this beautiful woman ever leave her carefully formed community and join him in the urban swirl of contemporary America? This collision of cultures is at least part of the drama of the film.

In one scene, a group of Amish head into the village in their buggies for supplies. They are goaded by some village tough guys trying to pick a fight, fully aware that the Amish are pacifist. As one of the bullies smears an ice cream cone into the face of a young Amish man, Book can resist no longer. He jumps out of the buggy and smashes him in the nose.

I first saw this movie in a theater, and at this point the audience erupted into applause. We wanted victory over the perpetrators of this demeaning injustice. But "this is not our way," one of the elders keeps saying to Book. The elder almost whispers, "We call down blessings on our persecutors, not curses."

Is it possible these simple people might teach us something about a radical way of human flourishing that is grounded in Scripture? What would our world look like if we formed communities that carried even a hint of what we witnessed in the Nickel Mines community's reaction to violence? Amish communities are shaped by living in the rhythms of our holy text, by living according to the patterns of its stories. The text is read and recited and repeated and sung over and over again until the Christian story proclaims itself, right in the midst of colliding stories, as a way of life that leads to human flourishing.

We also need to do the hard work of placing the holy Scriptures at the center of who we are as Christian universities. The challenge is not only that academic and secular culture would regard such a strategy as strange and ludicrous, but also that Christian culture seems to have lost its ability to teach the Scriptures. I base some of these conclusions on the work of Christian Smith, who with Melinda Lundquist Denton has written *Soul Searching: The Religious and Spiritual Lives of American Teenagers*. This work of scholarship is also in documentary form in *Soul Searching: A Movie About Teenagers and God*.[3] These scholars and this film convincingly make the point that this generation of students, predominantly Christian kids, simply does not know much about the Bible. Smith and Denton have produced a significant and convincing body of research that shows that Christian young people today don't have a language of faith because they have not been taught that language through a community of faith. They simply don't know the holy texts of their faith.

One teenager in Smith's book says, "You can believe whatever you want to believe. Like if somebody wanted to be a witch or something, they could study that and decide what they want to do."[4] Here is evidence of the deep cultural impulse that says we are all responsible for

---

[3]*Soul Searching: A Movie About Teenagers and God*, DVD, directed by Michael Eaton and Timothy Eaton (Revelation Studios, 2007).
[4]Christian Smith with Melinda Lundquist Denton, *Soul Searching: The Religious and Spiritual Lives of American Teenagers* (Oxford: Oxford University Press, 2005), p. 14.

our own maps. There seems to be little to guide us in deciding whether
one map is more credible than another. The tools of discernment are
missing. Even as the individual is encouraged to make choices about
faith from the wide array of options, there is huge reluctance to judge,
and there are simply no tools for making a choice about what is better
and what is worse.

"The point here is not that U.S. teenagers are dumb or deplorable.
They are not," Smith says.[5] "Many teenagers know abundant details
about the lives of favorite musicians and television stars or about what
it takes to get into a good college, but most are not very clear on who
Moses and Jesus were." To be sure, "nobody expects adolescents to be
sophisticated theologians,"[6] but when we listen in as they tell their
stories of faith, we get the picture pretty quickly that they do not have
very many handles with which to understand their faith tradition or
Scriptures. "Our distinct impression," Smith says, "is that very many
religious congregations and communities of faith in the United States
are failing rather badly in religiously engaging and educating their
youth."[7] Of course, this makes it very difficult for the Christian university to place the Scriptures at the center of its identity.

The focus is on the individual choosing a faith and pulling from that
faith tradition what seems useful. "For most teens," Smith writes,

> nobody has to do anything in life, including anything to do with reli-
> gion. "Whatever" is just fine, if that's what a person wants. Conse-
> quently, certain traditional religious languages and vocabularies of
> commitment, duty, faithfulness, obedience, calling, obligation, ac-
> countability, and ties to the past are nearly completely absent from the
> discourse of U.S. teenagers. Instead, religion is presumed to be some-
> thing that individuals choose and must reaffirm for themselves based
> on their present and ongoing personal felt needs and preferences."[8]

I must emphasize again that most of the students interviewed in this
study and in the documentary are religious kids, kids from Christian

---

[5]Ibid., p. 143.
[6]Ibid., p. 137.
[7]Ibid., p. 262.
[8]Ibid., pp. 143-44.

homes, kids from our churches. These are the kids who are coming into our Christian universities.

"The idea that one's life is being formed and transformed by the power of a historical religious tradition can be nearly incomprehensible" to these teenagers, says Smith.[9] Teens believe that

individuals must freely choose their own religion; that the individual is the authority over religion and not vice versa; that religion need not be practiced in and by a community; that no person may exercise judgments about or attempt to change the faith of other people; and that religious beliefs are ultimately interchangeable insofar as what matters is not the integrity of a belief system but the comfortability of the individual holding specific religious beliefs.[10]

These are alarming conclusions about our Christian young people, and all of this shapes up to be perhaps the most significant challenge we face as Christian universities: how to model for our students and for the world a genuine embrace of Christian Scriptures.

We must accept the challenge of creating vibrant Christian communities that provide for these young people a universe that "is not derived from one's own life" as the only source of meaning and direction. We must model for them the notion that "significance rather emanates" to individuals by becoming

connected to this larger moral order. . . . A morally significant universe . . . [that] provides individuals the big script of a very real drama, in the sense both that the story is intensely dramatic and that the drama is reality, within which the living out of one's life really means something significant because of the role it somehow plays in helping to perform the larger dramatic narrative.[11]

This is precisely our challenge as Christian universities: to create for our students, faculty and staff the communities where we read and study the Scriptures in such a way that we are swept up in God's huge drama of significance and order and ultimate meaning.

---

[9]Ibid., p. 144.
[10]Ibid., p. 147.
[11]Ibid., p. 157.

16

MODELING VIBRANT CHRISTIAN COMMUNITY

We must entertain each other in brotherly affection. . . . We must delight in each other; make others' condition our own; rejoice together, mourn together, labor and suffer together, always having before our eyes our commission and community in the work, as members of the same body. So shall we keep the unity of the spirit in the bond of peace.

JOHN WINTHROP

If Christians cannot extend grace through faithful presence, within the body of believers, they will not be able to extend grace to those outside.

JAMES DAVISON HUNTER

ONE OF THE MOST SIGNIFICANT WAYS the Christian university can engage culture and bring about change in the world is by modeling what I call *grace-filled community*. We do that modeling because it is right and good to live in community. Historically the university has sought to be a community of learners, confident that learning takes place best in community. We model community for our students so they too will move on into their lives to build strong and healthy communities. As we live in grace-filled community, we make an announcement to the world that there is another way of living and working together. As James Davison Hunter rightly says, "If Christians cannot extend grace through faithful presence, *within* the body of believers, they will not be able to extend grace to those outside."[1]

So much out of our great Christian tradition calls us to this goal for the Christian university. Despite some of our tendencies in American Christianity toward highly individualized faith, the teachings of the Scriptures and the compelling witness from the whole span of Christian history offer up a rich and varied call to community. In these communities of faith, grace and trust "we learn forgiveness and humility, practice kindness, hospitality, and charity, grow in patience and wisdom, and become clothed in compassion, gentleness, and joy. This is the crucible within which Christian holiness is forged," Hunter writes.[2] As we look around us, we see that the disintegration of community is one of the main sources of our contemporary grief—and so the modeling of healthy Christian community is a powerful tool for bringing about change.

———————————————— ▪ ————————————————

Where do we find in our Christian tradition the mandate and model for building communities of grace and trust and love? First, of course, the Christian Scriptures are exceedingly clear about the need for Christian community. Among any number of rich biblical texts, Paul's emphatic instructions to the followers of the new way in Rome might stand as a beginning point:

> Let love of the Christian community show itself in mutual affection. Esteem others more highly than yourself. With unflagging zeal, aglow with the Spirit, serve the Lord. Let hope keep you joyful; in trouble stand firm; persist in prayer; contribute to the needs of God's people, and practice hospitality. . . . Rejoice with those who rejoice, weep with those who weep. Live in agreement with one another. Do not be proud, but be ready to mix with humble people. Do not keep thinking how

---

[1]James Davison Hunter, *To Change the World: The Irony, Tragedy, and Possibility of Christianity in the Late Modern World* (New York: Oxford University Press, 2010), p. 244.
[2]Ibid., p. 253.

wise you are. . . . If possible, so far as it lies with you, live at peace with all. (Romans 12:10-13, 15-16, 18)

We all know this takes work and it takes perseverance in the task. It takes the shaping of a vision for this kind of community. It takes discipline and a continual defining of the habits of the heart and the habits of living together. It takes leadership as well as the commitment of everyone within the community.

Can we imagine a world operating on the basis of these principles? If not the world, then perhaps we could start at least by imagining communities of grace and trust and kindness in our Christian universities. If we can get an image of such a university in our minds, we can see our way toward a vision for our fractured and splintered world. Only then can we begin to sculpt a model of a Christian university that influences our world.

Throughout his letter to the Romans, Paul calls his followers to open their hearts to the transforming grace of God in Jesus Christ. In Christ we are reconciled to God. We become new people, profoundly changed. But it must be abundantly clear, Paul says, that we are reconciled to each other as well. Too often, when Christians have looked at a passage such as this from Romans, our tendency is to put the emphasis on individual behavior. We hear the words "let hope keep you joyful; in trouble stand firm; persist in prayer," and we interpret them in personal terms. But what if these standards of behavior stand also for the communities we are charged to build? Hope and joy and steadfastness and persistence in prayer—these are the marks of healthy Christian community too.

Personal commitment is prominent throughout the Scriptures, but as our lives are reconciled to God, we must change the way we live. I love the title of N. T. Wright's book *After You Believe: Why Christian Character Matters*. After we come to belief, character formation is the critical next step. But notice that personal formation is done *in community*. Community formation is essential to character formation. There is a sense in this passage from Romans that without community, personal formation may not even be possible. In addition, as we individually form these habits of the heart, we contribute to the formation of Christian community. And so "let love of the Christian community show itself" in all we do: Practice hospitality, show humility. Be kind and gracious, peaceful and joyful. These are the acts that form Christian community. This is what we must model in the Christian university we are imagining.

Wright says, "Imagine living in a community where, day by day, the normal habit of life for most people includes immorality, bad temper, jealousy, factions, envy, and so on." There are communities all around us in this frightful state. Sometimes we even find ourselves trapped in one—an organization, a company, a government office, a school or, yes, even a university. No one wants to live in these kinds of communities. They damage lives, diminish human potential, contribute to unhealthy stress and, in the end, create cynicism and pessimism.

But then, Wright adds, "imagine living in a community where, day by day, the normal habit of life is patience, kindness, gentleness, and self-control—not to mention love, joy, and peace."[3] Now, *this* is the way we want to live and work, isn't it? And it is exactly the kind of community the Scriptures call us to build: flourishing, grace-filled communities.

Think for a moment about how wonderful it is—or would be—to live in a community like the one described in Romans 12 and in biblical texts like it. Living in such community is a radical way to live and work, a satisfying way. "Those people know how to get along. They've got something going for themselves that is remarkable, unusual, good"— these are the words we want to hear about our Christian communities and Christian universities.

■

So that is the biblical call to community. Now let's look at some of the models of vibrant community we find throughout Christian history.

Some years before Dietrich Bonhoeffer was summoned to be executed at the Nazi concentration camp in Flossenburg, Germany, he offered up a celebration of Christian community in his marvelous little

---

[3]N. T. Wright, *After You Believe: Why Christian Character Matters* (New York: HarperOne, 2010), p. 207.

book *Life Together*. In 1938, as the ugly storm clouds of danger swirled around his small band of Christians, Bonhoeffer was wonderfully caught up in the joy and privilege of living in Christian community. What a text to guide our work in the Christian university!

"How inexhaustible are the riches," Bonhoeffer writes, "that open up for those who by God's will are privileged to live in the daily fellowship of life with other Christians!"[4] As I try to imagine what Bonhoeffer and his colleagues and friends were facing, and as I listen to his exuberant expression of the joy of living in community, I am ashamed that I don't work harder to build community. How can we let anything stand in our way? How can we tolerate in ourselves behavior that works against the vitality of "the daily fellowship of life with other Christians"? What a privilege, Bonhoeffer says. Oh the inexhaustible richness!

We need to fall on our knees, Bonhoeffer says in so many words, and thank God for the grace that allows us to gather in genuine community as Christians—even as we face the threat of dehumanizing hatred and even death. Let us gather together. Let us worship and pray together. And let us show kindness and love for one another. In this way, we may live with this kind of joy. In this way we can actually resist the threatening forces that surround us. We might even change this complex and dangerous world.

———————————————— ■ ————————————————

Over the years I have found myself turning to the Christian monastic tradition of the Middle Ages as a source for understanding genuine community. We might be under the impression that these extraordinary communities were excessively separatist, and in some ways they were. They were often located in isolated places, and they often practiced a fiercely protected self-sufficiency. But if we read their history with care, we find a profound and surprising openness to the world. Even as they defined such distinctive separated communities, their influence often reached out into the surrounding communities, even

---

[4]Dietrich Bonhoeffer, *Life Together: A Discussion of Christian Fellowship* (New York: Harper & Row, 1954), p. 20.

across the landscape of a fragile Europe. It can be argued that these little monastic communities literally changed the world.

As these peculiar monks and nuns sought to define a clear identity for their communities, they found the deepest resource of teaching in Christian Scripture. But it doesn't take long to recognize that they also enthusiastically reached all the way back to the rich texts of classical antiquity and the teaching throughout time of the Christian fathers. We see in them an impulse to read and study, to memorize, to preserve and collect, and to disseminate those important texts. There was no fear of broad learning. Grounded most of all in the Scriptures, these communities eagerly and joyfully opened themselves to all learning, the best of what had been thought and written. They approached learning fearlessly, just as they welcomed the outside world with hospitality and generosity.

We find in the monastic model two sides of a carefully worked-out balance: There was a profound turning inward, a persistent focus on the great texts that would define their identity, chief among them the Scriptures. They needed to define their way of life and the standards of their behavior according to those texts. But there was also a fearless openness to the world and to the known pagan texts outside the circle of their faith tradition. This was not a damaging separatism, but the fruitful practice of identity, from which they could be a model for the world around them. I submit that this is the balance that must define the healthy Christian community for our time, and indeed a model for the Christian university.

In his study of monastic culture, *The Love of Learning and the Desire for God*, Jean Leclercq demonstrates that the monks of the Middle Ages shared an optimism about life and the world. They studied the Scriptures *trustingly*, and then they looked at the world *hopefully*. Theirs was an "optimism [that] consists in thinking that everything true or good or simply beautiful that was said, even by pagans, belongs to the Christians," Leclercq writes. "This fundamentally Christian culture avails itself in the realm of expression as well as in the realm of the inner life, of antiquity's human experiences."[5] The monks made use of all learn-

---

[5]Jean Leclercq, *The Love of Learning and the Desire for God: A Study of Monastic Culture* (New York: Fordham University Press, 1961), p. 116.

ing. They loved learning. They were *not afraid*, and because of this, rather than practicing a separatism that discourages learning and kills the vitality of community, their exuberance brought life and vibrancy to their communities—and beyond.

The monastic tradition nurtured "holy imagination." These monks sought a "sanctification of the imagination." Leclercq says that, in our time, "our imagination, having become lazy, seldom allows us to do anything but dream." But for these monks and nuns of the Middle Ages, the imagination "was vigorous and active."[6]

Of course we must turn to the grand model of monasticism, St. Benedict. Benedict, an Italian born around 480, was the founder of a global monastic movement that remains vital to this day. His brilliant and ever-fascinating work *The Rule* was written around 530 at the Abbey of Monte Cassino. I suggest that this text might stand as an important guide for our aspirations toward Christian community in the university.

As a young man, Benedict left home in Umbria to go to school in Rome. Somewhere on this journey, he had a Damascus-road encounter with the living Christ. His heart, like Paul's, was transformed and his imagination was blown wide open to new possibilities. From that point forward he looked at the world with different glasses, and what he saw was a disintegrating Roman culture, with all kinds of decadent and destructive behavior. He saw chaos and the looming destruction of civilization, and he was appalled and frightened. Benedict decided the only hope was to withdraw from Roman society. With chaos and confusion swirling all around, he was able to imagine a community of order and health that might counter the forces of disintegration.

Benedict at first set off to become a hermit. Perhaps this singular pursuit of devotion to God could bring peace at least to his inner world. But as we read *The Rule*, we see Benedict's powerful attraction to Christian community, even while he remains informed by the practices of contemplative discipline. He recognized that devotion to God is not done by the individual alone, but in the study of Scriptures in commu-

---

[6]Ibid., p. 75.

nity, in worship together around the holy text of Christian Scriptures. In *The Rule*, Benedict captures some of the most compelling and enduring instructions for living in community ever written. It is a guide for leaders of community. It is a guide for living in community of any sort. It is a guide for the kind of community that is formed and shaped by the Christian Scriptures.

Some historians have claimed that the monastic movement saved Europe. Right in the face of the chaos and disintegration that followed on the heels of the collapse of the Roman Empire, "without a doubt, the monasteries had at times exerted such great influence that all Christian society lived, more or less, in the light they diffused," Leclercq writes.[7] James Davison Hunter adds this: "The monks were a cultural vanguard, and the monasteries they founded were strong institutions and culturally more developed than anything that existed in Celtic, German, Slavic, and Frankish paganism and culture."[8] The influence of these monasteries to save European civilization and contribute to the shaping of non-Christian, Greco-Roman civilization was enormous.

We may seem to be a long way away from our effort to define the work of the Christian university for our time. But think what might happen when we take seriously, as did these monasteries, the mandate of Scripture to build communities of trust and joy and grace. What might happen as we shine the light of these kinds of communities into the world, communities that are animated from the center by the Christian story, communities that worship together, communities that take seriously the reading of Scripture together? What might happen if we took seriously the study and preservation of deep and broad learning of the ages?

·

Let's shift gears one more time, this time to the seventeenth century and the ragged shores of unsettled New England. Here we find yet another model of Christian community. In 1630, about seven hundred

---

[7]Ibid., p. 256.
[8]Hunter, *To Change the World*, p. 58.

Puritans set off from England to establish a new way of life, to define a new model. John Winthrop was their leader, a man of broad learning and deep Christian conviction. To be sure, there was also a practical reason for their bold venture: England had been hit by severe economic depression, and these people were suffering hardship. Winthrop himself had discovered there was nothing left of his father's estate to inherit.

The Puritans' incredible journey was framed by brutal economic necessity, quixotic idealism and some parts utter foolishness—but they carried a vision that they were participating in God's sweeping drama that covered the whole globe. They believed they could be part of a plan and a promise to establish a human community that could flourish and prosper, a community that was guided by and centered on Scripture.

At some point along the way, this band of Puritan visionaries began to believe they could craft a new vision for a new society. They believed they could literally change the world, that they could model a new way of flourishing in human community. They could be a beacon of light for the entire world. They saw an opportunity to design and ultimately to model a new kind of community, a new way of living, a model taking its direction from Christian Scriptures.

With hindsight, we know the tragic limitations of their vision, including a fundamental inability to absorb into their consciousness the native people living on the land they hoped to settle. Their vision for human community was not big enough, as we look back, and much of that encounter is a shameful stain on our history. Wouldn't it have been marvelous had they been able to change the map of their culture, even in that moment of conflict and confrontation with native residents, to welcome into their understanding the powerful mandate of reconciliation with all people? What a lesson this is as we seek to take our own vision of the hope of the gospel into the world: We must watch out for the traps of our own culturally limited understanding of the gospel. We must carry the gospel always with humility.

Even so, Winthrop reflected on the possibilities of a new society based on the principles of Christian community. He echoed the admonition of Paul to the Corinthians or the Romans. Look to the history of the church "in all the ages," Winthrop said to his followers. What we find is "the sweet sympathy of affections which was in the members of this body one towards another." The only way to "avoid shipwreck" and see their experiment succeed was to

> entertain each other in brotherly affection, [to be] willing to abridge ourselves of our superfluities, for the supply of other's necessities. We must uphold a familiar commerce together in all meekness, gentleness, patience, and liberality. We must delight in each other, make other's conditions our own, rejoice together, mourn together, labor and suffer together.[9]

In other words, our experiment will fail miserably if we do not do the tough and necessary work, the rewarding work, of Christian community formation.

But how do we make such love a "habit in the soul"? It's going to be very difficult to "avoid shipwreck" on this venture of ours, Winthrop kept telling his shipmates. We are launching out on a very idealistic vision of settling a new land. We are trying to change the world. Can we do it? Will we succeed? What will it take to keep us on track? Only by committing ourselves to the arduous task, modeled throughout Christian history and mandated by the very Scriptures we hold dear, of Christian community formation. Only by making grace-filled community the "habit in the soul," only by "framing these affections of love in the heart" will we succeed.

Winthrop knows that the stakes for such commitment to community are very high. If they succeed, Winthrop concludes, "the Lord will be our God, and delight to dwell among us as His own people, and will command a blessing upon us in all our ways." If they would do the hard work of forming such a community of love and grace, "He shall make us a praise and glory that men and women shall say of succeeding plantations, 'the Lord make it like that of New England.'"

Others would look in on their experiment and see that it works.

---

[9]John Winthrop, "A Model of Christian Charity," in *The Norton Anthology of American Literature,* vol. 1, ed. Ronald Gottesman et al. (New York: Norton, 1979), pp. 23-24.

Others would look in and say, "Wow, those people know how to get along. They understand how to live together. Those people just might have a chance to change the world."

Here then is the ultimate concern for Winthrop, as for any Christian community: "For we must consider that we shall be a city upon a hill. The eyes of all people are upon us." If we fail to adopt such love, civility and kindness for one another; if we fail at our aspiration to model grace-filled community; if we fail to let the Scriptures transform the way we live and work and learn together, well, "we shall be made a story and by-word through the world."[10]

At the very heart of our vision to make the world a better place, Christian community is among the deepest of our commitments and aspirations. Modeling Christian community is at the heart of our influence on the world. Without it, we will not succeed. If we are modeling disdain for each other, politicizing our interactions, practicing bitterness, envy and bickering, we will have no chance of being a positive influence in the world. The world is watching, as Winthrop was so aware. We cannot blow it. If we sustain our commitment to modeling grace-filled community, the Christian university just might be the place where world change begins.

---

[10]Ibid.

17

AN ALTERNATIVE HISTORY,
AN ALTERNATIVE UNIVERSITY

> *If Christians are people with an alternative history*
> *of judgments about what is true and good*
> *they cannot help but produce an alternative university.*
>
> STANLEY HAUERWAS

EARLIER IN THIS BOOK WE SPENT A FAIR amount of time focusing on Stanley Fish's position that we must exclude the truth claims of religion from the discourse of the American academy. In many ways, despite small trends to the contrary, Fish's view of the purpose of the university has now become a kind of orthodoxy of our day. You can't study religion or treat the Bible as a great piece of literature, for example, because "the truth claims of a religion—at least of religions like Christianity, Judaism, and Islam—are not incidental to its identity; they *are* its identity." Take the truth claims out of the study of religion "and all you have is an empty shell, an ancient video game starring a robed superhero who parts the waters of the Red Sea, followed by another who brings people back from the dead." So, Fish rightly contends, "If you are going to cut the heart out of something, why teach it at all?"[1]

To teach the Bible's claim that God will make all things right in the end, for example, the great promise that is the anchor of Christian hope, to acknowledge such a truth claim at the table of discussion in the university is to allow "the camel's nose under the tent," and sooner

---

[1]Stanley Fish, "Religion Without Truth," *The New York Times*, March 31, 2007, sec. A15.

or later we might "turn the tent into a revival meeting," Fish says.[2] And nothing apparently could be more offensive to the operative definition of the purpose of the university.

But things are perhaps shifting. In an honest and more recent article, Fish admits there is a "growing recognition in many sectors that religion as a force motivating action could no longer be sequestered in the private sphere."[3] There is, he says, a "growing awareness of the difficulty, if not impossibility, of keeping the old boundaries in place and of quarantining the religious impulse in the safe houses of the church, the synagogue, and the mosque."[4] Over the past few years, we have become aware "that hundreds of millions of people in the world do not observe the distinction between the private and the public or between belief and knowledge, and that it is no longer possible for us to regard such persons as quaintly pre-modern or as the needy recipients of our saving (an ironic word) wisdom."[5]

This is an incredible shift in thinking for the formidable secularist Stanley Fish. He goes on to note that, on the campus where he teaches, "there are 27 religious organizations for students." Or just, "announce a course with 'religion' in the title, and you will have an overflow population."[6] The whole camel is already in the tent. Students apparently are lining up with people all over the world, saying without reservation that religion matters to them. There is a yearning to understand faith, faith traditions and the power of faith to form culture. Students get this. These things matter, and the university can go on seeking to exclude the sheer fact of faith or religion in the lives of people to its own detriment, its own loss of credibility.

"When Jacques Derrida died," Fish concludes, "I was called by a reporter who wanted to know what would succeed high theory and the triumvirate of race, gender, and class as the center of intellectual energy

---

[2]Ibid.
[3]Stanley Fish, "One University, Under God?" *Chronicle of Higher Education* 51, no. 18 (January 7, 2005): sec. C4.
[4]Ibid.
[5]Ibid.
[6]Ibid.

in the academy. I answered like a shot: religion."[7]

Time magazine ran a cover article on teaching the Bible in schools, arguing the need to retain our cultural grounding in these ancient texts that have shaped Western life over centuries. The article's author, *Time*'s senior religion editor David Van Biema, was most certainly not in favor of teaching anything approaching religion, but he did assert that the Bible is important again, now that we are losing touch with its formative stories.[8]

Stephen Prothero, chairman of the Department of Religion at Boston University, has received a lot of attention for his book *Religious Literacy: What Every American Needs to Know—and Doesn't,* a book about teaching religion in the public schools. He argues that we are experiencing religious illiteracy that must be addressed if our students are to understand the world in which we live. Not only do we need to understand other religions, but we must also understand the deepest strands of our own culture that are rooted in the Christian tradition.[9]

■

And so there is a shift going on, a belated and grudging recognition that religion matters to people across the globe and that our educational institutions ignore that fact to our peril. But let's not hold our breath. Radical change for the secular university regarding serious study of religion does not appear on the horizon, despite some signals of new openness.

Let's look, for example, at what happened when Harvard attempted to revise its general education program. When Larry Summers became president of Harvard in 2001, he announced that reform in undergraduate education was one of his top priorities. There seemed to be widespread agreement among faculty and students that the "core program," adopted in the 1970s, had grown tired, dated, even obsolete. The *Har-*

---

[7]Ibid.

[8]David Van Biema, "The Case for Teaching the Bible," *Time*, March 22, 2007, p. 40.

[9]Stephen Prothero, *Religious Literacy: What Every American Needs to Know–and Doesn't* (San Francisco: HarperSanFrancisco, 2007).

vard Crimson characterized this important project of general education revision as an attempt to "emphasize the real-world applications of a liberal arts education." In other words, Harvard sought to bring the core curriculum required of all undergraduates into alignment with the changing world in which we live.[10]

When the faculty committee released its "Preliminary Report" in October 2006, the real issues began to erupt, perhaps with surprising force. This first draft of the report proposed to recognize the study of religion as part of the new, required curriculum. In defense of the inclusion of religion, the "Preliminary Report" took note of the importance of religion in our world and among the very students Harvard serves.

> Religion is a fact of twenty-first-century life—around the world and right at home. Ninety-four percent of Harvard's incoming students report that they discuss religion "frequently" or "occasionally," and seventy-one percent say that they attend religious services. When they get to college, students often struggle—sometimes for the first time in their lives—to sort out the relationship between their own beliefs and practices, the different beliefs and practices of fellow students, and the profoundly secular and intellectual world of the academy itself.[11]

"The profoundly secular and intellectual world of the academy itself"—these are the words of the authors of the "Preliminary Report." Harvard's faculty struggled with a reality in the very halls of their prestigious university: Religion is important to students! It is important to students at all our universities, and it is important around the world. And so the authors of the "Preliminary Report" propose that the new core curriculum at Harvard include among its requirements a course on "Reason and Faith."

Just to make sure no one gets the wrong impression about this proposed requirement, the "Report" quickly adds, "Let us be clear. Courses

---

[10]Johannah S. Cornblatt and Samuel P. Jacobs, "Professors Approve General Education," *Harvard Crimson*, May 15, 2007 <www.thecrimson.com/article/2007/5/15/professors-approve-general-education-the-faculty/>.

[11]Harvard University Faculty of Arts and Sciences, "Preliminary Report," October 2006, p. 18 <www.sp07.umd.edu/HarvardGeneralEducationReport.pdf>.

in Reason and Faith are not religious apologetics. They are courses that examine the interplay between religion and various aspects of national and/or international culture and society." Fair enough, for Harvard or any secular university of our day. The goal is "to help students become more informed and reflective citizens. . . . Harvard is no longer an institution with a religious mission," and yet "religion is a fact that Harvard's graduates will confront in their lives both in and after college."[12]

Once the "Preliminary Report" was out in October 2006, all hell indeed broke loose. The eruption was not based on the usual difficulties any faculty has agreeing on the requirements of general education. No, this fierce debate is what happens when religion is introduced as a viable topic of meaningful and required learning in secular higher education. Should students be required to recognize religion as important to the world in which we live? Should the university recognize this global fact by requiring students to master some level of competency in understanding religion? Is this a competency necessary to negotiate the world in which we live? Those were the kinds of questions that created the stir.

Stephen Pinker, a psychology professor at Harvard, might be considered a representative of the resistance. He was worked up in part because of the importance of this process of curricular change at Harvard. "The final report will attract wide attention in academia and in the press," Pinker said, "where it will be read not for its specific recommendations, but as a once-in-a-generation statement on the nature of higher education from the world's most prominent university." This is a nod to a widely stated notion: as Harvard goes, so goes the rest of higher education in America.

But it is critically important to be clear here, says Pinker: "The word 'faith' in this and many other contexts is a euphemism for 'religion.' . . . A university should not try to hide what it is studying in warm-and-fuzzy code words."[13] The report makes it sound like the juxtaposition

---

[12]Ibid., p. 19.
[13]Stephen Pinker, "Less Faith, More Reason," *Harvard Crimson*, October 27, 2006 <www.the crimson.com/article/2006/10/27/less-faith-more-reason-there-is/>.

of faith and reason "are parallel and equivalent ways of knowing," and nothing, as Pinker sees it, could be further from the truth.

Pinker writes that "universities are about reason, pure and simple. Faith—believing something without good reasons to do so—has no place in anything but a religious institution, and our society has no shortage of these."

> For us to magnify the significance of religion as a topic equivalent in scope to all of science, all of culture, or all of world history and current affairs, is to give it far too much prominence. It is an American anachronism, I think, in an era in which the rest of the West is moving beyond it.[14]

And here is the crux of the matter. Really, has the "rest of the West" moved beyond considering religion as important in the lives of people and the culture that surrounds us? And what about the rest of the world, a world beyond the West, to which the academy prides itself in paying such ardent attention? What about the students of Harvard? Since the majority profess to be engaged with questions of faith and religion, are we to ignore the very people we serve? It sounds as if it is our task as a university to disabuse these students of their silly notions of faith, to make sure that reason, separated from faith, is the dominant mode of understanding for them, and that reason, of course, will displace the importance of faith once they see the light.

Pinker's position won the day, of course. In our day we have become accustomed to such conclusions. The final report on the general education reform for Harvard undergraduates eliminated "reason and faith" as a required component of the core curriculum. Contrary to the apparent importance of religion around the world, contrary to the evidence that Harvard undergraduates yearn to know more, faith has been cut from the list of what is essential for the graduate of this esteemed institution as they enter the world.

"In a world where faith shapes everything," John Schmalzbauer said in the *Wall Street Journal* just after the final report was issued, "from international relations to presidential elections, it is hard to argue with

---

[14]Ibid.

the idea that everybody ought to know something about religion." And yet, he says, "that is exactly what Harvard's faculty did."[15] They airbrushed the need to understand religion right off the map of the educational enterprise. This is precisely where the American academy begins to lose its credibility.

===================== ■ =====================

In his helpful book *The State of the University: Academic Knowledges and the Knowledge of God*, Stanley Hauerwas argues that theology ought to be recognized as a legitimate, vital, perhaps overarching discipline, even within the secular university. But while making his case with passion and elegance, Hauerwas is both skeptical and ambivalent about this prospect in the university as we know it. "I cannot nor do I wish to deny," he writes, "that the position I develop in this book is ambiguous."[16] I think Hauerwas knows his proposals will never really take hold in the secular university, though he wishes mightily that they would.

Hauerwas says with what must be tremendous regret that "theology is thought to be at best not necessary for educating students and at worst a subject that cannot pass the epistemological standards necessary to be an academic subject."[17] In the end, this was Harvard's position. How sad. How limiting. How out of sync with the rest of the world. How damaging to the deeper purpose of the university, damaging indeed to the credibility of the university. Those who claim for theology a place at the table of modern life and modern thought must recognize that "it is no secret that theology is no longer considered a necessary subject in the modern university."[18]

What are the consequences of this banishment of religion from the classrooms and curricula of universities? Hauerwas believes, as so many Christians have recognized for decades, that the university has caused

[15]John Schmalzbauer, "Harvard Loses Its Edge: Nixing a Religion Requirement Will Hurt the University," *Wall Street Journal*, December 15, 2006, sec. W17.
[16]Stanley Hauerwas, *The State of the University: Academic Knowledges and the Knowledge of God* (Oxford: Blackwell, 2007), p. 8.
[17]Ibid., p. 13.
[18]Ibid., p. 12.

great harm to its graduates, perhaps especially to those who are Christians. "I think it would be a mistake," Hauerwas says, "not to take seriously that what many learned, or thought they were learning, in colleges and universities led them to abandon Christianity."[19] For many in the secular academy this is a positive outcome, this disabusing students of their dogmatism, thereby opening their minds. But really, is this the outcome we should prize?

What a damaging indictment from the perspective of Christian students and families, those who come with the desire to know the truth, those who come embracing the Christian story and wondering how higher learning will help them better understand and articulate their story. But isn't this also damaging to students who are not Christians? Hauerwas says with some wistfulness "that students took course after course in which there was no discernible connection to Christian claims about the way things are surely created the conditions that made the conclusion that Christianity is at best irrelevant, and at worst false, hard to avoid." Students encounter in the secular university "knowledges that seem to make it impossible for them to think that what Christians believe could be true."[20]

The challenge is perhaps an epistemological one for all students. At best students end up assuming that the church may be important for spiritual or moral issues, but those spheres of life are not assumed to be about truth. At the core of the university lies an epistemology, an educational strategy, antithetical to the Christian story of what is true and good and beautiful. Entertain that story in private, they are told—in gatherings for Christian students, for example—but don't pretend that any such view can be allowed at the table of the real discourse of the university, where more truthful things are discussed.

For this and other reasons, Hauerwas says, "I obviously think that the university as we know it is in deep trouble." But then he quickly interjects, with typical ambivalence, "That does not mean we would be better off without the university."[21]

---

[19]Ibid., p. 47.
[20]Ibid.
[21]Ibid., p. 32.

So where do we turn? Here in part is the answer Hauerwas provides: "If Christians are people with an alternative history of judgments about what is true and good they cannot help but produce an alternative university."[22] Well, indeed! I agree wholeheartedly. I have enthusiastically embraced the Christian story as the story of what is true and good for my own life. In the decidedly secular culture in which we live, this is a choice for an alternative. We most certainly live in a profoundly pluralist world. We must recognize we do indeed live in a post-Christian world. But sadly, I have chosen to embrace a story that is essentially banished from the universities of our day. What then am I to do? My only choice is to articulate and endorse and lead "an alternative university." With what I hope is a position of humility and respect for the broader academy, I unhitched my commitments to the secular university a long time ago. We need an alternative! The alternative is the Christian university I am seeking to define in these pages.

While I prize the university as a force in our society; while I can trumpet the accomplishments of research and advancement of knowledge from those universities; while I have enormous respect for colleagues, friends and noted scholars who teach and do their life's work in a secular university as Christians; and while I will come to the defense, publicly and often, of the university in our society today—I have come to believe that the secular university is not providing for our students or for our society a coherent and whole story of what is true and good and beautiful.

We find skepticism in such able voices as Hauerwas, who says, "Please know I am not trying to argue for something called the Christian University."[23] Against such skepticism, I *am* arguing for "something called the Christian University." Indeed, I believe it is out of the work of the Christian university that we have the best hope to lead the way toward a vision for a better world.

I wish for Stanley Hauerwas, and so many others I greatly admire, all the best with the challenges within secular universities. May they keep speaking with their able and credible voices at the table of the

---

[22]Ibid., p. 91.
[23]Ibid., p. 7.

university. But for me, I have staked my claim on the Christian university, rightly conceived and at its best, as the best hope for learning in a world of colliding maps. Indeed I believe the Christian university can be the place where world change begins.

18

A STORY OF HUMAN FLOURISHING
AND THE WORK OF THE UNIVERSITY

The gospel of Jesus points us and indeed urges us to be
at the leading edge of the whole culture.

N. T. WRIGHT

The world is full of all kinds of possibilities, namely all the possibilities
of the God of hope. [We] see reality and mankind in the hand
of him whose voice calls into history from its end, saying,
"Behold, I make all things new," and from hearing this word
of the promise it acquires the freedom to renew life here
and to change the face of the world.

JURGEN MOLTMANN

IN JOHN HENRY NEWMAN'S GREAT discourses, delivered to a distin-
guished audience of educators and citizens in Dublin in 1852 and collected under the title *The Idea of a University*, we find some of the most
formative thinking about the nature of the modern university ever written. Throughout these extraordinary speeches, Newman engaged the
question of what place theology ought to occupy in the modern university. To say the least, Newman was troubled, even in 1852, that theology was being pushed to the side. He says, "it is the fashion just now, as
you very well know, to erect so-called Universities, without making any
provision in them at all for Theological chairs." With some measure of

amazement, he contends that "institutions of this kind exist both here and in England."

This "seems to me an intellectual absurdity," Newman writes, because "the very name of University is inconsistent with restrictions of any kind."[1] If we are true to our commitment to academic freedom, we must open a spot at the table of academic discourse for theology. Academic freedom? To be sure. A legitimate place for Christian theology at the table of discourse? Well, we think not. How can such a discrepancy exist?

Newman spots a disturbing cultural trend to separate theology and the Christian faith from what are considered more viable ways of looking at what is true. "Religion is excluded from a University course of instruction," Newman says, "not simply because the exclusion cannot be helped, from political or social obstacles, but because it has no business there at all, because it is to be considered a taste, sentiment, opinion, and nothing more."[2]

This is the great divide, the great separation or bifurcation that has set in over time. It is the presumed separation of what we regard as fact and what we deem to be "merely" matters of faith. The realm of belief, so the argument goes, must be allocated to mere personal preference, to be indulged only in the private sphere. "Well, it's okay for you to believe whatever you want, but just keep it to yourself," our culture admonishes us sternly. "Your theological reflections and positions are certainly your own business, but they are decidedly not the business of the university or of public discourse." Theology should be excluded from the university, the culture of Newman's day was already saying, though "it should be permitted in private, wherever a sufficient number of persons is found to desire it."[3]

"In a state of society such as ours," Newman asks, "in which authority, prescription, tradition, habit, moral instinct, and the divine influences go for nothing," how can we ever again locate and affirm a story

---

[1]John Henry Newman, *The Idea of a University* (Notre Dame: University of Notre Dame Press, 1982), pp. 14-15.
[2]Ibid., p. 24.
[3]Ibid., p. 33.

of what is true, a story that informs the very work of the university?[4] This is an astounding statement. Remember, Newman is writing this in 1852. Congruent with Newman's fears, in our day even more, when all authority, tradition and "moral instinct," and certainly anything we might call "divine influences"—when all this has been airbrushed out of sight, how in the world might we be guided by our ancient Christian story in our universities? We will not, of course, unless we imagine and create an alternative university.

Newman goes on to ask a critically important question: Might theology help? Can we really afford as a society to banish theology from discourse about things that matter? Does theology really "cast no light upon history? Has it no influence upon the principles of ethics? Is it without any sort of bearing on physics, metaphysics, and political science? Can we drop it out of the circle of knowledge, without allowing . . . that that circle is thereby mutilated?"[5]

To withdraw theology from our universities "is to impair the completeness and to invalidate the trustworthiness of all that is actually taught in them," Newman concludes. "Religious Truth is not only a portion, but a condition of general knowledge. To blot it out is nothing short, if I may so speak, of unraveling the web of University Teaching."[6]

This is an extraordinary assessment of the viability and credibility of a university curriculum in our day. It is extraordinary in part because it was written in 1852, just as the great sweep of secularization was beginning to settle into the culture. But it is also extraordinary because Newman began to sketch out the limitations, the huge gaping inadequacies, of the university without theological reflection on a guiding story of what is true and good and beautiful.

Eliminating theological insight from the larger considerations of human life, human community, human destiny, indeed the very earth itself, is to render knowledge "mutilated," distorted, incomplete, limited. What we teach is incomplete and untrustworthy. We are not telling the whole story to our students and to the world. We are offering

---

[4]Ibid., p. 28.
[5]Ibid., p. 50.
[6]Ibid., pp. 52-53.

them a stone instead of bread. Something is missing, something critically important to a full consideration of knowledge, insight and wisdom. We must be able to ask for something more.

——————————————— ▪ ———————————————

And so—theology matters. But how do we restore theological reading of Christian Scripture as the animating center of the work of the university? In *The Challenge of Jesus*, N. T. Wright makes a very important statement: "Our task, as image-bearing, God-loving, Christ-shaped, Spirit-filled Christians, following Christ and shaping our world, is to announce redemption to the world that has discovered its fallenness, to announce healing to the world that has discovered its brokenness, to proclaim love and trust to the world that knows only exploitation, fear, and suspicion."[7]

Wright is writing about Christians in general, but what if we were to adopt this statement as the vision statement for the Christian university? We have a chance—"following Christ and shaping our world"—to announce redemption, healing, love and trust to a fallen, broken, exploited, fearful, suspicious world. We do indeed have a story to tell, a story that is immensely relevant to the burning issues of our day. It is a story of human redemption, the profound promise that despite our fallenness and failure, one day all things will be made right. This is the hope we have to offer.

Wright goes on to say, with language that calls on precisely the unique tools of the university, that

> the gospel of Jesus points us and indeed urges us to be at the leading edge of the whole culture, articulating in story and music and art and philosophy and education and poetry and politics and theology and even, heaven help us, biblical studies, a worldview that will mount the historically rooted Christian challenge to both modernity and postmodernity, leading the way into the post-postmodern world with joy and humor and gentleness and good judgment and true wisdom.

---

[7]N. T. Wright, *The Challenge of Jesus: Rediscovering Who Jesus Was and Is* (Downers Grove, Ill.: InterVarsity Press, 1999), p. 184.

Wright says about our postmodern world that "you can't trust any-thing"; "you have to be suspicious of everything." Such a posture is pervasive and deeply ingrained into each of us, perhaps especially our students and our universities. Our great challenge, then, is to discover again that "there is such a thing as love, a knowing, a hermeneutic of trust rather than suspicion, which is what we most surely need as we enter the twenty-first century."[8]

Wright has his finger squarely on both the presuppositions of our culture and the call to action within the Christian story. And what an extraordinary call it is: To announce—right in the face of suspicion and the absence of trust—redemption and healing and love to a broken world. Such an announcement is guided by the trusting embrace of a story that gives coherence and meaning to the chaos we experience daily. We have such a story to offer.

But should this be the purpose of the university? My answer is de-cidedly yes. Of course. We must organize our work as Christian uni-versities around this story of healing and redemption, hope and joy. We must come off the margins of our culture, effectively and winsomely, to make such an announcement. We must nurture confidence and cour-age to speak into a desperate culture. We must master the tools of cul-tural engagement, equipping ourselves to be "at the leading edge of the whole culture," through every discipline of the academy, engaging the culture with "the historically rooted Christian challenge." How utterly exciting! What a measure of hope we might bring to our world!

This implies, indeed demands, mastering the skills to understand the culture. We must also master the tools of theological consideration of our ancient story of human flourishing. We must turn to the theolo-gians and scholars of the Scriptures on our campuses to help guide the way. And then, as Wright encourages us, we must address the world, not with arrogance and shrill confrontation, but "with joy and humor and gentleness and good judgment and true wisdom." This must be the work of our Christian universities. This is the Christian university at work in a post-Christian world.

---

[8]Ibid., pp. 196-97.

■

For Jürgen Moltmann, the driving purpose of the Christian story is to bring hope into a world gripped by hopelessness. Our God is a God of promise, says Moltmann. Our whole posture toward life in the present is shaped by the ancient promise of God. In a courageous act of faith in the face of haunting suspicion and doubt, we accept that God will make all things right in the end—as he has promised.

We are attentive, then, attuned to the signs that God is fulfilling his promise as the Christian story unfolds over time, throughout history, throughout our lives. We discover that story of promise over and over again, and we tell it over and over again. We tell the story in Christian community and in regular worship. We shout the story from the rooftops into our culture, into our broader communities, winsomely, wisely, effectively. I propose that this is the way our Christian universities must be shaped if we intend to be the place where world change begins. We must be people of hope.

Our hope comes from the promise that God will make all things right in the end. Justice will roll down, as the great Christian civil rights leader John Perkins is so fond of saying on my campus. Reconciliation is possible. Healing will happen. Peace will reign. Out of acute awareness of suffering and pain, disillusionment and hatred and dividedness—all things will be set right. This is the promise we claim as Christians, a promise that must shape all the work we do on the Christian university campus.

Christian universities must be universities of hope. Surely we cannot be universities full of suspicion, broken trust and hopelessness. What if hope is the radical, defining posture of our work? We can bring hope into the world, precisely because we see "the world is full of all kinds of possibilities," as Moltmann says, "namely all the possibilities of the God of hope."[9]

As a young German soldier in World War II, Moltmann was captured by the British. During his time as a prisoner of war, he began to

---

[9]Jürgen Moltmann, *Theology of Hope: On the Ground and the Implications of a Christian Eschatology* (1967; reprint, Minneapolis: Fortress, 1993), p. 26.

discover the horrors perpetrated on humanity through the brutal force of his own country. Someone gave him a Bible, and he began to explore for the first time a story of hope beyond the suffering and evil rumored back to his prison cell. He came out of his prison experience, on the one hand, with the horrors of the war swirling all around him, and on the other, carrying the transforming power of the gospel of hope. He devoted his life to live in the tension and to proclaim the God of promise, the God of hope. "The despairing surrender of hope," he goes on to say, "does not even need to have a desperate appearance. It can also be the mere tacit absence of meaning, prospects, future and purpose. It can wear the face of smiling resignation."[10]

Is this "face of smiling resignation" the gift we want to give our students, the gift with which we send them out into the world to make a difference? "Well, sorry," a graduate might say, "I have nothing to offer to a troubled world. I have no story of meaning, no story of human flourishing to offer, because I have learned, through my college education, that all such stories are called into question. In fact, I find myself cynical about all stories of hope. And so I say to the world, *Whatever. Beats me.* I will simply go about my business of making my life as comfortable as possible."

Resignation, suspicion and cynicism can never be the way for the Christian university to go about its business, because God has promised that we live in a world full of possibilities. We live in a charged, delightful, meaningful world, because we see reality and humanity, says Moltmann, "in the hand of him whose voice calls into history from its end, saying, 'Behold, I make all things new,' and from hearing this word of the promise [we] acquire the freedom to renew life here and to change the face of the world."[11] In other words, because we study and engage this world with vigor and attentiveness, equipped with the tools of engagement, we can face even the most hopeless of situations with hope.

"From first to last, and not merely in the epilogue," says this great theologian of hope, "Christianity is eschatology, is hope, forward look-

---

[10]Ibid., p. 24.
[11]Ibid., p. 26.

ing and forward moving, and therefore also revolutionizing and transforming the present."[12] I find in this hope of the gospel, as expressed in Moltmann's theology of hope, an animating purpose for the work of the university for our day. This is our call, isn't it? This is the promise we have to offer the world. This is what it means to be an alternative university animated by an alternative story of what is true and good and beautiful.

———————————————— ▪ ————————————————

Can a university change the world? If we turn to the theologians of our Scriptures and our faith tradition to help frame our purpose, indeed we can. Newman is right: If we drop theology and the theological consideration of our Scriptures "out of the circle of knowledge . . . that circle is thereby mutilated."[13] To withdraw theological insight from our universities "is to impair the completeness and to invalidate the trustworthiness of all that is actually taught."[14] We must enthusiastically invite our theologians and biblical scholars back to the table, at the very center of the enterprise, to provide a complete and trustworthy view of the world. They are the ones who might help us frame a vision of hope for the world.

This is the challenge of the Christian university for our day. If we can meaningfully and legitimately pull this off, I am convinced our Christian universities can become the place where world change begins.

---

[12]Ibid., p. 16.
[13]Newman, *The Idea of a University*, p. 50.
[14]Ibid., pp. 52-53.

CONCLUSION

Good philosophy must exist, if for no other reason,
because bad philosophy needs to be answered.

C. S. LEWIS

I believe we face the question: If not now, then when?
And if we are grasped by this vision, we may also hear the question:
If not us, then who? And if the gospel of Jesus is not
the key to this task, then what is?

N. T. WRIGHT

CONSIDER THIS STATEMENT BY POPE John Paul II: "The world, tired of ideology, is opening itself to the truth. The time has come when the splendor of this truth (*veritatis splendor*) has begun anew to illuminate the darkness of human existence."[1] What a profoundly hopeful statement. What a wonderful way to conclude our sometimes discouraging look at the destructive forces of a nihilistic culture of colliding maps. The Pope has an answer: The splendor of the truth we find in the gospel of Jesus Christ shines again into the darkness of our world.

John Paul II's statement speaks of deep *trust* in the power of *truth* to

---

[1]Pope John Paul II, *Crossing the Threshold of Hope* (New York: Knopf, 1994), pp. 164-65.

change our world. Of course this wise and thoughtful leader knew full well that the language of "truth" in our postmodern culture is so often burdened with debilitating complexities. Truth is problematic, we have come to understand. Truth according to whom? John Paul II knew full well he was engaging this culture of skepticism, yet he believed that the *truth* of the gospel might begin "anew to illuminate the darkness of human existence." Is it possible this very truth might set us free? Indeed, our confidence rests in this trust; world change begins in the light of the splendor of truth.

Do we dare share this compelling hope that the splendor of truth is shining into the darkness of human existence? We must. This must be our confidence. Indeed, the world is tired. The world is weary of the ideological conflicts that do so much damage to our lives and to the world; we indeed live in a world of colliding maps. Not all of God's children are flourishing. And our cultural habits of suspicion and denial keep us from providing viable alternatives.

We must ask a further question: Are we paralyzed in the face of "the darkness of human existence" because we have *no center of truth*? When there is no center, as Yeats tells us so vividly, "Things fall apart. . . . Mere anarchy is loosed upon the world."[2] So John Paul II is right: It is this center we yearn for, this splendor at the heart of it all. This is the path out of our weariness. This is the place where world change begins.

Is it possible that the world may be "opening itself to the truth" again? Surely we catch glimmers of that splendor shining through at times. We have seen through our poets some of those glimpses, some of the hints of this glorious splendor—the "grandeur of God," as Hopkins saw it. And we claim with some measure of confidence and trust that this very splendor of truth will shine once again into the darkness of our situation. This is our hope. This is the source of our confidence.

Is the world "opening itself up to the truth"? The answer must be emphatically yes, even in the midst of the tired and destructive splin-

---

[2]William Butler Yeats, "The Second Coming," *Selected Poems and Two Plays of William Butler Yeats*, ed. M. L. Rosenthal (New York: Collier Books, 1962), p. 91.

tering to which our ideologies have brought us. The answer must be yes for every Christian who claims—as the Gospel of John announces so eloquently, so *truthfully*—that in Jesus Christ there is life, and in that life we find the light of the world. The answer is yes as we claim the great promise of this splendor: This light, this very splendor of truth, shines in the darkness, and the darkness will never overcome it![3]

But then we must ask this question: Where do we find institutions that are animated from the core by this very splendor of truth? My answer? I believe the Christian university can be a model for just this kind of institution. The various and distinct universities we call Christian universities—scattered out across our country, so many of them established over a hundred years ago, each of them rooted by a very unique history—these universities have the chance to be the place where the splendor of truth shines out with joy and radiance and hope.

I have tried to outline the ways this splendor can shape the Christian university. We have talked about the need to become culture experts, for example, so that we can equip our students to be culture-savvy, so that we may conduct our scholarship as cultural engagement. We must learn to speak the language of culture, even as we call that culture to a new, life-giving way.

We have talked about adopting the power of the imagination to break out of the fixed notions of our culture. Through the imagination—in the tradition of the biblical imagination—we have a chance to shatter the confinement and restrictions forced on us by philosophical materialism, for example, and break out of the limitations of anything less than expansive vision for our lives and our world.

We have sought to imagine how we might embrace the Christian Scriptures at the heart of university life, becoming biblically and theologically educated, even in a time of biblical illiteracy and theo-

---

[3]Paraphrased from the opening of the Gospel of John.

logical shallowness. We have sought to outline the power of cultivating life together in genuine, grace-filled community, to understand the shaping influence of worshiping in community, to lift up the profound witness of modeling communities of trust, grace and reconciliation.

All of this represents a great deal of hard work and requires strong leadership and the collective wisdom of vibrant Christian scholars, theologians, teachers, students and supporters. Together we can build an institution that is illuminated by the splendor of truth, an institution capable of shining the light of our compelling Christian story of human flourishing into the world.

∎

As millions of people mourned the passing of John Paul II on April 2, 2005, and during the days that followed, we witnessed not just respect and love for this great leader, but also a yearning and a hunger for something like the splendor of truth, for a release from the weariness of divisive ideology. George Weigel, the author of the Pope's biography, *Witness to Hope*, said in the *Wall Street Journal* that Pope John Paul II continued to affirm throughout his life the "inviolable mystery of the human person." At the core of his teaching was a deep, unshakable conviction, profoundly informed by the splendor of truth, that all human life has dignity—the unborn and the little children, the poor and the rich, the educated and the uneducated—all of God's children deserve to live in communities of human flourishing.

It was out of this conviction, Weigel says, that John Paul II kept calling for "vibrant public moral cultures capable of disciplining and directing the tremendous energies—economic, political, aesthetic, and, yes, sexual—set loose in free societies."[4] As we too are guided by this splendor of truth, our universities must seek to build such cultures. This is precisely what we have tried to imagine for the Christian university of our day.

---

[4]George Weigel, "Mourning and Remembrance," *Wall Street Journal*, April 4, 2005, sec. A14.

■

In October 1939, as the Nazis brutally invaded Poland, C. S. Lewis asked a very important question about the life of the university: Did his beloved Oxford have anything relevant and helpful to say about these horrifying global developments? Should the university be addressing issues such as war and freedom and sovereignty, or should the university sit this one out on the comfortable margins? Did the university have anything to say about the evil unleashed across the landscape of Europe? And what was the university doing to equip its students to become graduates who actually might change this frightening world? Lewis believed the university was on the defensive, and he felt challenged to define its very reason to exist for such a time as this.

One Sunday evening during that tumultuous October, Lewis preached a sermon to a standing-room-only audience of students and faculty at the Church of St. Mary the Virgin on the Oxford University campus. While the future of European civilization seemed to hang in the balance, Lewis asked his audience "whether there is really any legitimate place for the activities of the scholar in a world such as this."[5] Of course this is the vital question we must ask of the university at every moment in history.

A debate going on in England at the time tilted in the direction of pacifism, optimism and isolationism. Winston Churchill found himself embattled out on the margins as he began to argue for a forceful stand against the looming threat of Hitler and the Nazis. So many voiced the opinion, among them some of the great scholars of the academy, that Hitler would come around at last toward peaceful reconciliation and resolution. In 1933, the historian Paul Johnson tells us, as Hitler took power in Germany, many in the public square believed that he would be seen "as a deluded adventurer who would soon be discarded." In fact, the Oxford Union, consisting of all the undergraduates of Oxford, took a vote and overwhelmingly declared "that this House refuses in any circumstances to fight for King and Country."

---

[5]C. S. Lewis, "Learning in War-Time," *The Weight of Glory: And Other Addresses* (New York: Collier, 1949), p. 22.

To the students of Oxford, in the comfort and privilege of their ivory tower, there seemed to be no need to resist the dark forces sweeping across Europe. For Churchill, this was a sign of the irrelevance of the academy. He called the vote of the Oxford Union "that abject, squalid, shameless avowal . . . a very disquieting and disgusting symptom."[6] He saw such a vote as a declaration of withdrawal into irrelevance.

And so on that evening in October 1939, when Lewis gave his sermon, the stakes were very high. The British were called on to measure their course of action. Every leader needed to take a stand, including academic leaders and undergraduates at Oxford. The countries of Central and Eastern Europe had taken "the first sip, the first foretaste of a bitter cup which will be proffered to us year by year," Churchill said, "unless by a supreme recovery of moral health and martial vigour, we arise and take our stand for freedom."[7] The question for Lewis and others at Oxford was where the university would stand.

Lewis began to build his defense for the place of the university in a time of conflict: "To be ignorant and simple now is to capitulate to the forces behind the brutality and carnage we witness on the fields of battle."[8] High levels of competency are required in a dangerous world. The venture of learning must be profoundly connected and responsive to exactly the forces we witness in our world. We must know and understand what's going on in the world. We must be attentive. We must develop the skills and competencies to engage such unfolding and threatening forces at work in the world. We must be thoughtful and savvy. We must seek wisdom. Now is no time to be "ignorant and simple," to be sure. If what we see all around us is not acceptable in the broader scheme of human flourishing, the job of learning is to change things, to make things better rather than worse. These are the "weapons" the university must marshal to make the world a better place.

But it is not just competency and skill alone that matter in a dangerous world. While Lewis understood that the battles raging across Eu-

---

[6]Paul Johnson, *Churchill* (New York: Viking, 2009), p. 92.
[7]Ibid., p. 101.
[8]Lewis, "Learning in War-Time," p. 28.

rope must be answered with military resistance, the real battles were cultural, philosophical and ultimately religious. Churchill called it a recovery of "moral health." This is the battlefield where one view of the world is pitted against another. And this is where the tools of the university come into play—at least if we are rightly focused, at least if we are animated by a story of what is true and good and beautiful, at least if the splendor of truth shines out from our center.

And so Lewis offered an extraordinary definition of the purpose of the university for a troubled world: "Good philosophy must exist, if for no other reason, because bad philosophy needs to be answered."[9] In other words, the university matters profoundly in the struggle against the forces of destruction, *if* the university has a story to tell, a "good philosophy" that will counter and challenge "bad philosophy."

In a culture prone to call all philosophies morally equivalent, how can we take up Lewis's challenge of discovering, crafting and embracing something we affirm with assurance to be "good philosophy"— against "bad philosophy"?

This is our answer to the struggle of our complex and troubled world. It is the only way to counter the forces that lead to death instead of life. Discovering, shaping and articulating "good philosophy" is where world change begins, and it is in our universities—at least the universities with an alternative history of what is true and good and beautiful—where this good philosophy can be studied and articulated and taught.

———————————— ■ ————————————

Closer to our own time, N. T. Wright asks this provocative question: "How can the stories by which so many have lived have let us down? . . . How shall we replace our deeply ambiguous cultural symbols? What should we be doing in our world now that every dream of progress is stamped with the word Babel?"[10] In the pages of this book, we have

[9]Ibid.
[10]N. T. Wright, *The Challenge of Jesus: Rediscovering Who Jesus Was and Is* (Downers Grove, Ill.: InterVarsity Press, 1999), p. 172.

tried to examine the stories of culture that have "let us down." We have tried to think about "what we should be doing" to engage such a culture *so that* we might announce to the world a powerful alternative story. Wright goes on to ask,

> Did you never hear that [God] created the world wisely? And that he has now acted within his world to create a truly human people? And that from within this people he came to live as a truly human person? And that in his own death he dealt with evil once and for all? And that he is even now at work, by his own Spirit, to create a new human family in which repentance and forgiveness of sins are the order of the day, and so to challenge and overturn the rule of war, sex, money, and power?[11]

This is the alternative story of what is true and good and beautiful. Christians are a people defined by this story. How can we embrace this story within our Christian universities? How can this story become the animating center of who we are as universities? And then—even in this post-Christian world in which we live and do our work—how can we announce to the world this story of human flourishing? These are the questions we have been addressing in these pages. This is how we become a place where world change begins.

Sociologist James Davison Hunter observes that "to be Christian is to be obliged to engage the world, pursuing God's restorative purposes over all of life, individual and corporate, public and private."[12] In these pages we have accepted this definition of how to be a Christian in our world. We are called to be "world-makers," Hunter says.[13] But let us clearly understand the source of our vision for human flourishing. Hunter adds,

> When the word of all flourishing—defined by the love of Christ—becomes flesh in us, in our relations with others, within the tasks we are given, and within our sphere of influence—absence gives way to presence, and the word we speak to each other and to the world becomes

---

[11]Ibid.

[12]James Davison Hunter, *To Change the World: The Irony, Tragedy, and Possibility of Christianity in the Late Modern World* (New York: Oxford University Press, 2010), p. 4.

[13]Ibid., p. 3.

authentic and trustworthy. This is the heart of a theology of faithful presence.[14]

I claim this "theology of faithful presence" for the Christian university I have been imagining. Faithful presence is the mark of incarnation. And it is the path to human flourishing, the place and the practice where world change begins. We must define our purpose as Christians and as Christian universities as a "commitment to the new city commons" and recognize this as "a commitment of the community of faith to the highest ideals and practices of human flourishing in a pluralistic world."[15] What an exciting venture this is—to be such active participants in God's grand drama of hope for his world!

Hunter ends his book with a reflection on Jeremiah's vision about how to live world-shaping lives even in exile. Jeremiah wrote to all those among God's people who were banished from their homeland, exiled in seeming hopelessness to Babylon. Exile can bring bitterness, resignation, confusion—everything we have observed about life in our own time. But take heart, Jeremiah says, because our God is a God of promise. God will make all things right in the end. In the meantime, here is what you should do:

> Build houses and live in them; plant gardens and eat the produce; marry wives and rear families; choose wives for your sons and give your daughters to husbands, so that they may bear sons and daughters. Increase there and do not dwindle away. Seek the welfare of any city to which I have exiled you, and pray to the Lord for it; on its welfare your welfare will depend. (Jeremiah 29:5-7)

In other words, model a flourishing life even in the midst of exile. Model vibrant communities of trust, grace and love. Build decent lives and healthy families and thriving communities. And contribute to the welfare of the city in which you are exiled. As Hunter says, "For Jeremiah, exile did not mean that God had abandoned Israel. Rather, exile was the place where God was at work."[16]

---

[14]Ibid., p. 252.
[15]Ibid., p. 279.
[16]Ibid., p. 277.

━━━━━━━━━━━━━━━━━━━━━━━━━━━━ ∎ ━━━━━━━━━━━━━━━━━━━━━━━━━━━━

And so, finally, can a Christian university change the world? N. T. Wright ends his book *The Challenge of Jesus* saying, "I have been particularly concerned to put into the minds, hearts and hands of the next generation of thinking Christians the Jesus-shaped model of, and motivation for, a mission that will transform our world in the power of Jesus' gospel."[17] This is the task I have attempted as well. This is the task, I believe, of the Christian university for our day.

"The substance and structure of the different aspects of our world need to be interrogated in the light of the unique achievement of Jesus," Wright continues. This is the work of the Christian university: to engage the culture, to interrogate the culture in the light of Jesus and then to be agents of transformation. This is what it means to engage the culture and change the world. This is what it means to be the Christian university in a post-Christian world.

This is our challenge, the challenge of Jesus, the challenge of the Christian university for our time. And I believe, with N. T. Wright again, that we face the question: "If not now, then when? And if we are grasped by this vision, we may also hear the question: If not us, then who? And if the gospel of Jesus is not the key to this task, then what is?"[18]

---

[17]Wright, *Challenge of Jesus*, p. 11.
[18]Ibid., pp. 184-96.

BIBLIOGRAPHY

Arendt, Hannah. *Between Past and Future: Eight Exercises in Political Thought*. New York: Penguin Books, 1961.

Arnold, Matthew, "Stanzas from the Grande Chartreuse." In *The Norton Anthology of English Literature*. Edited by M. H. Abrams et al. 6th ed. New York: Norton, 1996.

————. "Dover Beach." In *The Norton Anthology of English Literature*. Edited by M. H. Abrams et al. 6th ed. New York: Norton, 1996.

St. Benedict. *The Rule of St. Benedict*. New York: Vintage Books, 1981.

Berger, Peter. *A Rumor of Angels: Modern Society and the Rediscovery of the Supernatural*. New York: Doubleday, 1969.

Bonhoeffer, Dietrich. *Life Together: A Discussion of Christian Fellowship*. New York: Harper & Row, 1954.

Brooks, David. "Human Nature Today." *New York Times*, June 26, 2009, sec. A25.

————. "The Jagged World." *New York Times*, September 3, 2006, sec. C10.

————. "Moral Suicide a la Wolfe." *New York Times*, November 16, 2004, sec. A27.

————. "The Organization Kid." *Atlantic Monthly*, April 2001, p. 40.

Brueggemann, Walter. *Finally Comes the Poet: Daring Speech for Proclamation*. Minneapolis: Fortress, 1989.

————. *Hopeful Imagination: Prophetic Voices in Exile*. Philadelphia: Fortress, 1986.

Brown, Dan. *The Da Vinci Code: A Novel*. New York: Doubleday, 2003.

Burtchaell, James Tunstead. *The Dying of the Light: The Disengagement of Col-*

leges and Universities from Their Christian Churches. Grand Rapids: Eerdmans, 1998.

Cahill, Thomas. *How the Irish Saved Civilization: The Untold Story of Ireland's Heroic Role from the Fall of Rome to the Rise of Medieval Europe.* New York: Doubleday, 1995.

Carter, Stephen L. *The Culture of Disbelief: How American Law and Politics Trivialize Religious Devotion.* New York: Basic Books, 1993.

Casteen, John T., III. "Presidential Leadership." *The Presidency,* Fall 2002 <www.virginia.edu/presidentemeritus/spch/02/spch_presleadership.html>.

Charry, Ellen T. *By The Renewing of Your Minds: The Pastoral Function of Christian Doctrine.* Oxford: Oxford University Press, 1997.

Cornblatt, Johannah S., and Samuel P. Jacobs. "Professors Approve General Education." *The Harvard Crimson,* May 15, 2007 <www.thecrimson.com/article/2007/5/15/professors-approve-general-education-the-faculty/>.

Crouch, Andy. *Culture Making: Recovering Our Creative Culture.* Downers Grove, Ill.: InterVarsity Press, 2008.

Dockery, David. *Renewing Minds: Serving Church and Society Through Christian Higher Education.* Nashville: B & H Publishing, 2008.

Driscoll, Jeremy. "The Witness of Czeslaw Milosz." *First Things* 147 (November 2004): 28-33.

Eliot, T. S. *The Four Quartets.* New York: Harcourt, Brace & World, 1943.

———. *The Waste Land and Other Poems.* New York: Harcourt, Brace & World, 1930.

Fish, Stanley. "One University, Under God?" *Chronicle of Higher Education* 51, no. 18 (January 7, 2005): C1, C4.

———. "Religion Without Truth." *New York Times,* March 31, 2007, sec. A15.

———. *Save the World on Your Own Time.* New York: Oxford University Press, 2008.

———. "Stanley Fish Replies to Richard John Neuhaus." *First Things* 60 (February 1996): 27-34.

———. "Why We Can't All Just Get Along." *First Things* 60 (February 1996): 18-26.

Greenspan, Alan. *The Age of Turbulence: Adventures in a New World.* New York: Penguin Press, 2007.

Guroian, Vigen. "Dorm Brothel: The New Debauchery, and the Colleges

That Let It Happen." *Christianity Today*, February 2005, pp. 45-51.

Hauerwas, Stanley. *The State of the University: Academic Knowledges and the Knowledge of God.* Oxford: Blackwell, 2007.

Harvard University Faculty of Arts and Sciences. "Preliminary Report: Task Force on General Education." October 2006 <www.sp07.umd.edu/Harvard GeneralEducationReport.pdf>.

Hays, Richard B. *The Conversion of the Imagination: Paul as Interpreter of Israel's Scripture.* Grand Rapids: Eerdmans, 2005.

——. *First Corinthians: Interpretation, A Bible Commentary for Teaching and Preaching.* Louisville: John Knox Press, 1997.

Henry, Douglas V., and Michael D. Beaty, eds. *Christianity and the Soul of the University: Faith as a Foundation for Intellectual Community.* Grand Rapids: Baker Academic, 2006.

Holmes, Arthur F. *The Idea of a Christian College.* Grand Rapids: Eerdmans, 1987. First published in 1975.

Hopkins, Gerard Manley. "God's Grandeur." In *The Norton Anthology of English Literature.* Edited by M. H. Abrams et al. 6th ed. New York: Norton, 1996.

Hunter, James Davison. *The Death of Character: Moral Education in an Age Without Good or Evil.* New York: Basic Books, 2000.

——. *To Change the World: The Irony, Tragedy, and Possibility of Christianity in the Late Modern World.* New York: Oxford University Press, 2010.

Huntington, Samuel P. *The Clash of Civilizations and the Remaking of the World Order.* New York: Simon & Schuster, 1996.

Johnson, Paul. *Churchill.* New York: Viking, 2009.

Kolakowski, Leszek. *Modernity on Endless Trial.* Chicago: University of Chicago Press, 1990.

Krauss, Lawrence M. "Reason, Unfettered by Faith." *Chronicle of Higher Education*, January 12, 2007, sec. B20.

Kronman, Anthony T. *Education's End: Why Our Colleges and Universities Have Given Up on the Meaning of Life.* New Haven: Yale University Press, 2007.

Leclercq, Jean, OSB. *The Love of Learning and the Desire for God: A Study of Monastic Culture.* New York: Fordham University Press, 1961.

Lewis, C. S. "Learning In War-Time." *The Weight of Glory: And Other Addresses.* New York: Collier, 1949. Originally delivered as a sermon at St. Mary the Virgin Church in Oxford, October 22, 1939.

Litfin, Duane. *Conceiving the Christian College.* Grand Rapids: Eerdmans, 2004.

McCarthy, Cormac. *No Country for Old Men.* New York: Knopf, 2005.

McEwan, Ian. *Atonement.* New York: Anchor Books, 2001.

———. *Saturday.* New York: Doubleday, 2005.

MacIntyre, Alasdair. *After Virtue: A Study in Moral Theory.* Notre Dame: University of Notre Dame Press, 1981.

Mannoia, V. James, Jr. *Christian Liberal Arts: An Education That Goes Beyond.* Lanham, Md.: Rowman & Littlefield, 2000.

Marsden, George M. *The Soul of the American University: From Protestant Establishment to Established Nonbelief.* New York: Oxford University Press, 1994.

Miller, Eric. "Alone in the Academy." *First Things,* 140 (February 2004): 30-35.

Milosz, Czeslaw. *New and Collected Poems: 1931–2001.* New York: Harper-Collins, 2001.

———. *To Begin Where I Am: Selected Essays.* Edited by Bogdana Carpenter and Madeline G. Levine. New York: Farrar, Straus, Giroux, 2001.

Moltmann, Jürgen. *Theology of Hope: On the Ground and the Implications of a Christian Eschatology.* 1967. Reprint, Minneapolis: Fortress, 1993.

Mouw, Richard. "Critical Thinking." Fuller Theological Seminary President's Blog, June 18, 2007.

———. *Uncommon Decency: Christian Civility in an Uncivil World.* Downers Grove, Ill.: InterVarsity Press, 1992.

Newbigin, Lesslie. *Foolishness to the Greeks: The Gospel and Western Culture.* Grand Rapids: Eerdmans, 1986.

———. *The Gospel in a Pluralist Society.* Grand Rapids: Eerdmans, 1989.

———. *Proper Confidence: Faith, Doubt, and Certainty in Christian Discipleship.* Grand Rapids: Eerdmans, 1995.

Newman, John Henry. *The Idea of a University.* Notre Dame: University of Notre Dame Press, 1982.

Nietzsche, Friedrich. *The Portable Nietzsche.* Edited and translated by Walter Kaufmann. New York: Penguin Books, 1954.

Noonan, Peggy. "There's No Pill for This Kind of Depression." *Wall Street Journal,* March 13, 2009, sec. A9.

O'Connor, Flannery. *A Good Man Is Hard to Find and Other Stories.* New York: Harcourt Brace Jovanovich, 1955.

Pelikan, Jaroslav. *The Idea of the University: A Reexamination.* New Haven:

Yale University Press, 1992.

Pinker, Stephen. "Less Faith, More Reason." *Harvard Crimson*, October 27, 2006 <www.thecrimson.com/article/2006/10/27/less-faith-more-reason-there-is/>.

Pope John Paul II. *Crossing the Threshold of Hope.* New York: Knopf, 1994.

———. *"Ex Corde Ecclesiae,* On Catholic Universities." Encyclical Letter, 1990.

———. *"Veritatis Splendor* (The Splendor of Truth)." Encyclical Letter, 1993.

Potok, Chaim. *The Gift of Asher Lev.* New York: Ballantine Books, 1990.

Prothero, Stephen R. *Religious Literacy: What Every American Needs to Know—and Doesn't.* San Francisco: HarperSanFrancisco, 2007.

Schmalzbauer, John. "Harvard Loses Its Edge: Nixing a Religion Requirement Will Hurt the University." *Wall Street Journal*, December 15, 2006, sec. W17.

Schwehn, Mark R. *Exiles From Eden: Religion and the Academic Vocation in America.* Oxford: Oxford University Press, 1993.

Shelley, Percy Bysshe. "A Defence of Poetry." In *The Norton Anthology of English Literature.* Edited by M. H. Abrams et al. 3rd ed. New York: Norton, 1974.

Smith, Christian, with Melinda Lundquist Denton. *Soul Searching: The Religious and Spiritual Lives of American Teenagers.* Oxford: Oxford University Press, 2005.

Smith, James K. A. *Desiring The Kingdom: Worship, Worldview, And Cultural Formation.* Grand Rapids: Baker Academic, 2009.

Sommerville, C. John. *The Decline of the Secular University.* Oxford: Oxford University Press, 2006.

Soul Searching: Teens and God. DVD. Directed by Michael Eaton and Timothy Eaton. Revelation Studios, 2007.

Steinfels, Peter. "At Commencement: A Call For Religious Literacy." *The New York Times*, May 12, 2007, sec. B6.

———. "Roberts Nomination Raises the Issue of the Role of Religious Faith in Public Life." *The New York Times*, July 30, 2005, sec. A13.

Taylor, Charles. *A Secular Age.* Cambridge, Mass.: Belknap Press of Harvard University Press, 2007.

Van Biema, David. "The Case for Teaching the Bible." *Time*, March 22, 2007, p. 40.

Volf, Miroslav. *Exclusion and Embrace: A Theological Exploration of Identity, Otherness, and Reconciliation.* Nashville: Abingdon, 1996.

Webber, Robert E. *Who Gets to Narrate the World? Contending for the Christian Story in an Age of Rivals.* Downers Grove, Ill.: InterVarsity Press, 2008.

Weigel, George, *The Cube and the Cathedral: Europe, America, and Politics Without God.* New York: Basic Books, 2005.

———. "Europe's Problem—and Ours." *First Things* 140 (February 2004): 18-25.

———. "Mourning and Remembrance." *Wall Street Journal*, April 4, 2005, sec. A14.

———. *Witness to Hope: The Biography of Pope John Paul II.* New York: Harper Collins, 1999.

Williams, William Carlos. *Selected Poems.* New York: A New Directions Paperbook, 1969.

Winthrop, John, "A Model of Christian Charity." *The Norton Anthology of American Literature.* Volume 1. Edited by Ronald Gottesman et al. New York: Norton, 1979.

Witherington, Ben, III. "Why 'The Lost Gospels' Lost Out." *Christianity Today,* June 2004, pp. 26-32.

Wolfe, Tom. *I Am Charlotte Simmons.* New York: Farrar, Straus, Giroux, 2004.

Wright, N. T. *After You Believe: Why Christian Character Matters.* New York: HarperOne, 2010.

———. *The Challenge of Jesus: Rediscovering Who Jesus Was and Is.* Downers Grove, Ill.: InterVarsity Press, 1999.

———. "Decoding *The Da Vinci Code.*" Address delivered at Seattle Pacific University for the President's Symposium on the Gospel and Cultural Engagement, Seattle, WA, May 18-19, 2005.

———. *The Last Word: Beyond the Bible Wars to a New Understanding of the Authority of Scripture.* New York: HarperSanFrancisco, 2005.

———. *Paul: In Fresh Perspective.* Minneapolis: Fortress, 2005.

———. *What Saint Paul Really Said: Was Paul of Tarsus the Real Founder of Christianity?* Grand Rapids: Eerdmans, 1997.

Wright, N. T., Robert Wall and Paul Sampley. *The New Interpreter's Bible.* Volume 10. "The Letter to the Romans." Nashville: Abingdon, 2002.

Yeats, William Butler. "The Second Coming." *Selected Poems and Two Plays of William Butler Yeats.* Edited by M. L. Rosenthal. New York: Collier Books, 1962.

Index